Align with your Angels

Awaken your inner power, wisdom and joy.

AUDREY CLARKE

BALBOA.PRESS
A DIVISION OF HAY HOUSE

Balboa Press books may be ordered through booksellers or by contacting:

Balboa Press
A Division of Hay House
1663 Liberty Drive
Bloomington, IN 47403
www.balboapress.co.uk
UK TFN: 0800 0148647 (Toll Free inside the UK)
UK Local: (02) 0369 56325 (+44 20 3695 6325 from outside the UK)

Print information available on the last page.

ISBN: 979-8-7652-1623-1 (sc)
ISBN: 979-8-7652-1622-4 (e)

Library of Congress Control Number: 2025924803

Balboa Press rev. date: 01/26/2026

CONTENTS

Audrey's story vii

Part 1

Chapter 1 Angels are with you now 1
Chapter 2 The Nature of your existence 11
Chapter 3 Communication with your angels-
expanding your personal power 20
Chapter 4 Angel insights to the Law of Attraction 26
Chapter 5 Intention – Increasing your personal
powers of attraction 34
Chapter 6 Self Love, your highest intention 42
Chapter 7 Clearing the clutter, the first step 53
Chapter 8 A Blueprint to connection-Steps to tuning
into your angelic guidance 59
Chapter 9 Meditations to connect you to your angels
and your Higher being 67

Part 2 - Questions and Answers

Chapter 10 About angels and how they help you 85
Chapter 11 Angelic perceptions of humans 92
Chapter 12 The Universe from our viewpoint 106
Chapter 13 Karma and justice from an angelic perspective.. 120
Chapter 14 Current world challenges that can affect
your Vibration 130

Chapter 15 Applying angelic guidance to your life, your life purpose and self-development 136
Chapter 16 Overcoming relationships Issues with the angels..149
Chapter 17 Recalibrating Fear to Love 161
Chapter 18 Parenting with the angels..................................169
Chapter 19 Coping with loss and grief with help from your angels...177
Chapter 20 Angelic advice for challenging life situations 183
Chapter 21 Your Intuition is your guiding star 195
Chapter 22 Cultivating abundance with the angels 204
Chapter 23 Final Words...210

Appendix 1 215
Appendix 2...219
Appendix 3 221
Acknowledgements. 223
About the Author 225

AUDREY'S STORY

One night in September 2019 I awoke with a jolt and sat upright in bed. It was four in the morning. I could hear a voice in my right ear. I knew at that moment it was not my own. It asked me to get up and start writing. I left my bed and padded to the spare room where my red laptop was. I opened it up and words flowed out on to the screen, and I knew they were not my words.

What followed was astonishing to me. I began to type what I heard for the next ninety minutes. The words amassed easily on the screen. Over the course of the next few months, I got my early morning call to arise. It was consistently at four in the morning when I would awake. I felt compelled to keep writing at this time, as the information I was being given, was vastly different to anything I had ever encountered. Once I finished typing, I would read the text back and was consistently amazed at the information.

While it took a while to find out about the source of this latest information, I was assured from early on that it was a benevolent force. The words were always very kind, and they told me that I was important to them and that I was myself a powerful individual. This couldn't have been further than how I felt about myself at the time. I had been going through some health issues and as a busy mother of three children I felt that I was always failing at everything. There did not seem to be enough hours in the day for what I needed to do. I rarely gave myself any credit for anything. I felt overwhelmed and the sense of never being and doing enough. There was criticism in the house I grew up in, and I had taken this and internalised it. It had gotten so bad that I was not able to perceive the many ways in which I was helping my family, friends, and others. In short, I had lost sight of myself and my inherent worth and value as a person.

This voice was a force of positivity in my life encouraging me in any interests that I had and pointing out the ways I was uplifting others and making a difference in the world. After many nights of writing, I enquired as to who the voice belonged to. They told me they were a group of angels. For the first six months of our communication, I continued to rise early to type. Looking back on those words now I feel immense gratitude for the guidance that they gave me. I knew that on my part, discipline was necessary to show them I could be consistent. A key motivating factor was also that I was so curious as to what they would have to tell me. That insatiable curiosity was a driving force. After six months, I put more boundaries in place as to when I would write as I was becoming exhausted. As I had been writing consistently over this period, I was able to hear this voice at any time I wished to. I still find early mornings when I initially wake up to be the best time to tune in. I believe this is because there is less momentum going on and my mind is clearer.

On the first morning I spoke with my guides, I was told I would write a book with their messages for the world. As you can imagine this came a quite a shock as I hadn't so much written a poem at that time. I felt totally inadequate and doubted my capability to complete the task. I felt at the time they must have made a mistake, but I now realise there are no mistakes when working with angelic guides. I also felt curious and was intrigued at the prospect of hearing more from them which kept me turning up every day to hear their messages.

Here is one of the first messages I channeled from my guides in the Autumn of 2019.

Audrey, we send you love. We want you to know you are all divinely guided, and you can ask for assistance from us, your angels, at any time. If you tune in to us, we will give you the answers to any questions you have. This is because your higher being already knows the answers to all you desire. You didn't come into this world alone. Your higher being and angels guide you. We are with you always. When you connect with us life is much easier. When you act from your guidance you are open to all the abundance of the universe, and you are centred, whole and complete.

You are deeply loved by your non -physical guides and here are some things we would like for you

-to be peaceful and at ease.

-to know that it possible to live a full joyful life by living in the present moment.

-to be alive to all the possibilities of your life and to what you can manifest.

-to be aware that you are creating your life with your beliefs and thoughts, be it negatively or positively. Your thoughts create your experience.

-to be aware you can change your thoughts at any time and this can change your experience dramatically for the better. This is because of the law of attraction.

Over the course of five years of consistently writing their guidance, they have never failed to give me clarity and assistance on any topic that is important to me. I am deeply humbled to receive this guidance as I had often thought my problems were insignificant in the grand scheme of things. What I now believe is that we are all important in the eyes of source (God/Divinity). Everyone has their guide or guides with them. We are never alone. I am not special. This guidance is available to everyone, without exception. This book is about becoming more attuned to it. Clarity can be a game changer in life because your energy is cohesive in the direction that you are guided too. You begin to doubt yourself less and life begins to feel like it is happening for you not just happening to you.

In this book, which is channelled, with the help of my guides I will discuss what they want us to know at this time. I will talk about ways of becoming more in tune with your guidance and how to access clarity and wisdom from your guides daily. I will discuss my own path to being able to access the wisdom of my angelic guides in my life. The angels want us to know that this clarity and wisdom is available to everyone, no exceptions exist.

PART 1

CHAPTER 1

Angels are with you now

Who are we and how can we help you?

We are a group of non-physical guides that visit Audrey and help her with her creative endeavours. We are responsible for dictating the content of this book. We have given Audrey the name Jeronimo, but our name is not important or significant. She visualises us as a group of hooded individuals, much like monks, that come to her before she begins to write. Significantly we hand her a quill or feather to let her know we are present. Audrey continues to have her own guides, but we are visitors to help her with this project.

We came when Audrey had already started this work to help her continue it and get it over the line. We have been part of writing projects in the past that were important spiritually and that helped raise consciousness in the world. This is our goal with this text also. It is our great privilege to help to bring this information to you now. We have a deep love for all of humanity and want to help to raise the consciousness of the planet so a world that is based on love can be born. Love is the greatest force and in the universe. As humans, your capacity for love is unlimited, indeed when you limit your love for others you feel awful. Love is hardwired into your being, from the beginning of your existence to the present moment. It is your default option. The love that all of us in the non-physical realm have for you is so profound that if you were to allow yourself to feel even a small amount of it, for a moment, you would weep tears of joy. This love is your birthright and is here for you and we wish to show you how to access it. Ultimately love is our guiding star, our modus operandi and it is our intention that you will experience more love for yourself and others by reading this book. Any small expansion in your consciousness is a tremendous win for us. Those of us on the non-physical plane continue to envelop you in the purest love that we know will help raise your vibration and contribute to the expansion of your consciousness.

Angels your non-physical buddies

We are beings of the light and guardians of the Earth. It is our time to speak with you now as we have messages that can help the world as it is today. Our intention in starting this conversation is to bring knowledge to reassure and guide you. It is our primary aim to inform you of the love that the non-physical beings such as us, have for you. It is truly immense. We often wish you could see yourselves as we see you. We see you as magnificent divine beings. It has been said that you are made in the likeness of God and indeed this is true. The divine shines through you in your every cell.

Our viewpoint of the earth and its inhabitants is indeed a bird's eye view in that we are removed and at this distance there is more clarity. Also, as non-physical beings, we are lighter without the mass that you call the body. We are also removed from emotion. From our perspective, we can see the world, galaxies and the universe as a great living entity. We can see the subtleties at play at every level. We are a part of it yet detached from it so we can perceive the whole. We are aware of the secrets of this universe that are difficult to understand while you are in the physical dimension. This does not make us in any way superior to you. On the contrary, we admire those of you who have chosen to come back into this time and space continuum as we realise it is challenging to be alive in the world right now.

It is important to say that everything we have shared in this book has been written from our point of view. Our point of view is that we are existing in non-physical dimensions, and as a rule, have not incarnated on Earth or had experience of being physical. We have the perspective of appreciating the greater universe from where we are. We can understand and integrate the knowledge of the whole universe from our standpoint.

Our intention in bringing this material to you is to give you a greater perspective on the laws of universe and how they work in your daily life. Our key goal is to bring you into contact with your own angelic guides and your higher being who know everything that you desire in life and the path of least resistance to help you find it. We acknowledge that the human experience on Earth has it challenges but we see that sometimes, you make things more difficult for yourself, by putting attention on conditions, people and things that do not please you. By shifting your focus to more positive things, you can lift your vibration and attract things that are more pleasing to you. Focus is a currency; your social media platforms know this as they are vying constantly for your attention. You can choose where to put you focus and this is very much where your power lies.

Imparting Clarity in our own way.

Our style of answering questions may sometimes appear to be blunt. What we emphasise from our standpoint may not have occurred to you before. It is our highest intention to never cause you to blame yourself for anything negative that has happened in your life. While it is the case without exception, that you create your own experience, you co create with the universe, with your vibration being the vital component of this. You do not live in a vacuum and other people and situations can affect your vibration. It is multifaceted and you fluctuate in vibration all the time. We bring this information to you, so you realise that you have so much power over how your life turns out. This means you can truly create the conditions that please you if you are persistent in your focus. What has been created before no longer matters, your power is in the present moment and what you give your attention to is crucial.

We would like to point out the strategic use of repetition in this book. We are using it as a learning device. Bear with us if it times it seems tedious. We are not in any way inferring that your intellect cannot appreciate the concepts on first reading them. On the contrary, we know that you are intelligent and interested in self-growth and development which is why you were attracted to this book. It is our knowing that concepts can be better integrated when repeated and applied to different situations which is why we have structured this book in a question-and-answer format. It is our intention that it may help you integrate our teachings more effectively.

All parents know that repetition is a powerful teaching tool as they commonly sing the same songs to their children who gradually learn the words and join in. Hearing something repeated fires new neural connections in your brain and lays the pathways for absorbing and integrating new material. The concepts we discuss are from the non-physical perspective and may seem strange to you initially. We use repetition to enhance learning and understanding by adding layer upon layer like building a structure. We are always building on what we have previously said, but it may seem to you to be repetitive at times. This a deliberate tactic intended to help you learn in a structured way.

This book can be read in sequence or can be dipped in and

out of, depending on what resonates for you. If something piques your interest or is relevant to your life, we encourage you to re-read it. This is an effective way of integrating the information. We mention the term source God or Source throughout this book. This is to describe the universal intelligence that is present and was present when your world was created and while it evolved into what it is currently. We do not aspire to put forward a creationist or evolutionary explanation for the planet you are residing on, because the truth is complex. We want to assure you that the universal Source or God is kind and loving and very aware of you and your life. You are an important part of the evolution of the planet and without you the whole would be incomplete.

If you do not believe in God that will not dissipate the value of this book, for we discuss many ways to come into greater contact with your own personal power through the higher part of yourself or your higher being. If you can read this book with an open heart and mind it is our promise you will receive information that is comforting to you.

Key Concepts

1. You came into the physical world but a part of you remained in non-physical, your higher being.
2. You have had other lives and have reincarnated into this one.
3. When you decided to reincarnate into this life, you knew the conditions you would be returning to. Your chose to return, to this time space continuum, for learning and expansion.
4. The purpose of you being here is to learn and your expansion adds to the expansion of the universe.
5. You are never alone, and you have angelic guides with you always.

6. Your guides want to help you. They know exactly where you are currently and how best to help you get where you want to be.
7. It is possible to interact with your guides, and they are always willing to help.
8. All is one, we are all connected in this universe and are all a part of the greater matrix of energy or Source.
9. Energy flows where attention goes. What you put your focus on; you attract more of whether it be negative or positive.
10. There is no death, you continue to exist in a different energetic form after you leave your body.
11. Vibration is everything. You are emitting a vibration that influences everything that comes into your life. You can change your vibration.
12. You manifest and attract situations to your life through your thoughts and emotions. Your vibration is the ultimate deciding factor.
13. Because your vibration is responsible for what you attract it is important to care about how you feel. The better the feeling, the higher the vibration.
14. The law of attraction means that what is likened to itself is drawn or like attracts like.

Please do not stop reading this book now if you do not agree with the above concepts. We have put these first as a declaration of the perspective we have from the non-physical plane. It is normal to come your own conclusions through your experience of life. Experience is how you learn. Can you be open to allowing this material to be true for you? Go within and see how it sits in the body. For example, there may be huge resistance that comes up to the idea that all is one, if you were brought up to see others as different whether inferior or superior. We do not ask that you change your views to align with ours, but you can you just allow the possibility of what we are saying to be true for you. Even if you cannot now, we recommend you keep reading for more information on how we see the universe from our perspective. It is our intention to explain our position throughout this book clearly.

How to use this book

As your angels, we are pleased that you have come across this book. Our intention when writing this was to make you aware of the angelic guides that you have and to suggest ways in which you can be in touch with them. The meditation section will show you processes to come into communication with your guides. There is no recommended route through his book. The one that is most important is the one that appeals to you the most. Focus on what resonates with you.

With the meditations if you can take time during your day to complete any of them that appeals to you. There are many processes that can be employed, and they are described in detail. The bulk of the book is in question-and-answer format. This came about when we were initially answering questions that Audrey was curious about and it expanded into questions that relate to issues that people may be experiencing with life and relationships. We have covered a wide variety of issues and problems. There may be answers for you contained within even if the problem does not pertain directly to your life experience.

Even though we give general advice to Audrey, she finds that the specific guidance that we give her is the most helpful. The answers to the questions are from our viewpoint, that is, knowing what we know about the laws and make-up of the universe. It is from a broader point of view. We always want to acknowledge your magnificent and powerful nature. We are aiming to uplift with our answers which is always our intention. Please understand it may not correspond to what a friend might say because we are not in physical form and thus have a greater overview of the universe. We also come from a place of seeing the whole of your being not just the part that is in physical form on Earth currently. We are referring to your higher being which is the energetic part of you that remains in non-physical and has all the wisdom of your past lifetimes and a good understanding of the laws of the universe.

We have grouped the questions into broadly similar groups. We may answer questions in a similar fashion because we are teaching through repetition. This serves the purpose of driving home our core messages about vibration and the power of emotions. Repetition can be helpful when trying to embed new ideas and concepts. It does not require that you have the same world view as us to appreciate our answers. If you can be open to receiving the messages, then that is enough. We have intended to make our words as succinct as possible. Allow any feelings that arise and welcome and treat them with curiosity. We are speaking to an area at the core of your being that is wise and knowing. There is nothing new here, you already know this knowledge at a deeper level. Our aim is to bring the truth within you to light.

It can be helpful if something resonates with you to read it again. Taking time to digest and absorb the ideas within is wise. There is nothing complicated here. As Wayne Dyer said "when you change the way you look at things, the things you look at change." Just a simple adjustment in your thinking about anything can have the potential to transform what you attract into your life. You can choose to think that the world is full of helpful strangers, or you can believe it full of dangerous vicious people. In either case you will be right. It is what you think it is. Make room for positive thought in your life. Move to expecting the best from others and watch what happens. Use the power of intention to set the tone of your day. Work on your ability to receive and to appreciate the positive traits of others in your life. These may seem like insignificant things, but they are huge in influencing outcomes in your life.

There are those with vested interests in the world that would like to keep you powerless and small. They achieve this through media broadcasting terrible news regularly. We believe that focus is a form of currency. You can see that technology companies are vying for your focus with their multiple offerings. Is it any wonder that concentration spans are dropping dramatically. Your power is in the present moment. When your attention is divided then you are less powerful, and your manifestation power is diminished. This is something that can be remedied by incorporating meditation practices and bringing your attention back to focus on positive thoughts. At this time of strife in the world, it is even more important to come back to yourself and reclaim your personal power. We provide multiple processes for achieving this.

It is our intention with this book, to raise awareness to the existence of angels and how they can help you in your life. We hope that you will begin to appreciate that you are never alone and that you are constantly being guided. It is our hope that you will develop a personal relationship with your guides so that they may enhance your experience in life. They have so much to offer you if you can open your heart and allow their messages to come to you. It is a process, and it may be different for everyone. This very much depends on whether you learn visually, audibly, or kinaesthetically.

Do not worry if what we say does not resonate with you at times. If you can get a general sense of what we are communicating that will be sufficient. We promise you our words are not wasted on you and what we are saying is working on you on a deeper level. The words and energy in this book are high in vibration or in other words pure positive energy. It is our intention that it will offer you answers to your life's dilemmas and that you will take what you need to from it.

Why we asked Audrey to write this book now.

At this time in the world there is a lot of confusion and deliberate misleading of people via the social media platforms. This misinformation serves the purpose of fuelling fear and anxiety in people daily lives. When a person is operating out of a state of fear it is likely that they will remain stuck and disconnected from the possibility of new options for their life. Their personal power is greatly diminished when fear becomes predominant.

The information that we provide here is in opposition to this. We want to assure you that you are safe and guided from the moment you are born until you die. Also, you are part of all of creation and without, you it could not be whole. We want to point you to your personal power by highlighting the process of intending and the co-creation. The truth that you are connected to every living being on the planet is mentioned, so you can become aware that you are part of a greater whole. The simple truth that you are not alone and that you are loved by us and source God, can have the ability to transform your life and how you are in the world.

We want to become aware of your power and raise your vibration as by doing so you will add to the collective consciousness of the planet and play your part in global enlightenment. The payoff for you is that you can move forward in a dynamic fashion co-creating with the universe exactly what you desire. There is not time pressure because time as you know it on earth does not exist.

CHAPTER 2

The Nature of your existence

We are here to reassure you of the existence of a creator/source God/Goddess who cares about you on an intimate level. You are never alone in this world as you are always connected to Source. Guardian angels surround you. Your angels want to help and guide you and they love you. Often, they are not heard or perceived by you. We will explore ways to better connect with your guides later.

Your composition is not just the physical body that you can see today. You are a vibrational being as well as well as having a body composed of matter. When you came into this body, you were already existing in the non-physical realm. The entirety of your being in non-physical was a representation of all your experience and wisdom that you accrued from past lives and experiences. You decided to reincarnate into your body in this space time continuum. Most souls go forth for the experience of creating conditions that they will enjoy, fully aware that there may be contrasting experiences but safe in the knowledge that all experience leads to expansion of the being but also of the entire universe.

When you came into your body here on Earth, you slowed down your fast vibration to become matter in this world. However, only a part of the whole of you came into the body. The greater part of you did not and remains in the non-physical realm but connected to you. We call this your higher being. It is the greater part of you. This means that you are not just simply your body and the energy within your body. Your higher being has the records of all the lives you have lived and all the wisdom you have accrued in those lifetimes. It is a wonderful source of wisdom that you can draw on to help you in day-to-day life.

Your higher being knows where you are at and what you desire and knows the path of least resistance to get you there, as do we. Your higher being stays focused on you and is always beaming wisdom to you. It knows your strengths and your abilities and is loving and appreciating you so much because it has the view of the totality of your being which is magnificent. When you are in tune with your higher being you are in alignment with the whole of you. It feels like ease and flow. When you are thinking or acting out of alignment with your higher being it never feels good.

If there is one lesson that we teach that is most important it is this, become aligned with the whole of you (higher being) before you act. This multiplies the power of your action a hundredfold. It is important to frequently ask yourself under what influence am I acting? Stopping and quietening your mind can help you come into alignment. For others, it can be meditation. In time, you can develop this into a set of values that you act from but always being aware these values may change and shift.

As we have mentioned, you are a vibrational being in a vibrational universe. Also, that there is a greater part of you, your higher being. These are universal truths as best we can describe them in words. Of course, there is much more than what you can understand from your perspective in the physical world. When you have returned to non-physical all will be understood. You will be united with your higher being, on that plane, so your powers of cognition and understanding will be multiplied. A key goal of this book is that you can connect to your higher being and angelic guides. Meditations and processes will be described later in the book.

We can imagine that this information may be new to you, and this is ok however can you begin to allow it to settle within you. This is not something new, rather something that you are remembering. You already know this information at the core of your being. Even if it sounds fantastical, stay with us and we will describe how to connect to your higher being and us.

Why your angels want to connect with you now.

Perhaps the biggest fallacy that humans tell themselves is that they are alone. That they are born alone, and they will die alone and that all of life is meaningless. This could not be further from the truth. Your angel guides are with you from the time you come into this world. They never leave your side for the whole of your life and when you die, they help with your transition to the next world.

You do not have to believe this, and you can close this book and stop reading now if you wish. Your guides will still be with you and working behind the scenes for you whether you believe in them or not. The energy of the guides is always appreciative and loving and so they naturally want to connect with you. They never want to scare you or upset you in any way. It is your decision if you wish to connect with them and in what manner.

We feel that life as you know it would be easier on many levels if you knew that you have support from a non- physical source. We want you to know that we are always interested in your life. We want to offer our support, and we will suggest ways in this book that you can come into communication with us. This is something everyone can do without exception. You have an in-built system to access this guidance and support. Many are not aware of this, and most do not know how to go about accessing it. We will discuss this fully in the coming chapters.

We want to ensure this book is a how to, in relation to coming in to contact your guides and hearing their guidance. It is our intention that through reading this book and taking the actions suggested you will develop a relationship with your guides and your guardian angels. We wish to set out a set of practical skills that you can use to enhance this connection. This will be a simple step by step process that will help you tap into the power and clarity of your angels and guides. Forging a deeper connection to your angels can have profound effects on your life. It can be amazing to ask the guides and to have clarity on anything you desire in life. This is possible if you have the dedication to work to hear the guidance more thoroughly

Shifting self-perception to change what you attract.

As angelic guides, we wish to set the record straight as how you perceive yourself does have an impact on what you create in your life. When you change your beliefs, this can lead to desirable changes in your life. We want you to know that we keep you in our focus constantly so that we can help you. You can move away from it or close yourself off to it, but love is what you are. It is your true essence. This is not about perfection or being good enough, what this means is that we see you in your truest highest state which is pure love. This is the only way we see you. We do not believe the things you tell yourself about yourself, that are not loving.

Your thoughts about yourself are often harsh and judgemental. This also comes from conditioning from your society which likes to point out your flaws and places so many obstacles on your path to feeling good about yourself. We want you to know that we see you as you truly, magnificent beings. Indeed, if we were together, you would try and dissuade us from feeling this way about you.

You would point out a lengthy list of your flaws, faults and failing. You would say that you have made mistakes, and you are not perfect. Most of all you would say you are not deserving to be valued so highly. We wish to say, we could not see you as anything other than divine and magnificent. We will never take our focus off you. We will never hold you in our intention with anything other than unconditional love. We will always stay focused on your perfection and your potential. There is nothing that will ever deter us from this, for it is our function and in serving you we serve ourselves and the entire universe.

It is important to Source/God that the connection between you and your guides is enhanced. This time and space continuum is vibrating with a lot of heavy energy. There is a lot of fear in the general consciousness of the world. We want to speak to you of collective consciousness of the world. A great law of this universe is that we humans are all interconnected with each other and with the animal, plants and other species of the planet. This is a great truth also known as All is One. There is also something known as collective consciousness. This is the collection of thoughts of every being on the planet at this moment of time. As you can imagine looking at the current state of the world there is much fear and negativity in the collective consciousness currently leading to aggressions and wars. Every thought you have also contributes to the great collective consciousness also. In this way, it is in everyone's interests that we clear up our negative projections, so we do not add to the burden of negativity in the world. Does that sound like a tall order to you?

It may seem that you have no control over the thoughts that you are thinking but this is not true. This notion is dispelled when you realise that you are the observer of the thought. If you can step back from your thought a little. You can do this by sitting back into awareness and watching the thoughts as they occur. You can say to yourself I wonder what my next thought will be. You can rest in presence and observe what happens when the thought comes in. You may notice that the thought comes in and passes through making room for a new thought. In this scenario, you are the watcher of the thought. But who is watching the thought? It is your higher self or your I am presence. The great power in knowing you are the watcher of your thoughts is that it allows you to realise that you are not your thoughts. It means you can allow your thoughts to pass through without getting attached to them in any way. You can also begin to choose what thoughts you will think. This does not mean if you have a negative thought that you need to fight it or never think negative thoughts again. Of course, this is not possible. Almost all humans are inclined to think negative thoughts. It may be possible sometimes, to stop yourself before you get caught up in a negative thought loop. The law of attraction will draw more thoughts to them, whether they be negative or positive thoughts. Thus, the momentum of your thoughts matter when it comes to what you will create or manifest in your life.

Angels Interactions.

Your angels have come with you since your first day on this planet. They are here to provide help and guidance for you. It is possible to interact with your angel. Giving you resources to do so is the ultimate point of this book.

Angels are non-physical beings sent from source God to help you on your Earth Walk. This is true whether you believe it or not. Since the beginning of time humans have been perceiving the presence of angels. They are depicted in many great art works around the world. In art they can take the shape of a human with wings. We as Angels wish to say there is no specific way to perceive us. It can be in any way that is personal and meaningful to you. It is only recently Audrey can, with eyes closed, begin to perceive our shapes. A human eye or sense will always detect a human like appearance. It matters not what our true shape is. It is only important that you agree with the possibility of our existence. That is the starting point by which we can begin to work with you.

The love that source creator has for all their creations is immense and the most important message in this entire book is that you are not alone. You were not born alone, nor will you die alone. Angels are always with you. Everyone has their guardian angel with them for their entire time on Earth. It is true that other angels may come to help in time of hardship or despair or indeed creativity. For example, Audrey has the help of scribe angels in the process of transcribing this book.

You can become more attuned to the wisdom of your guides by meditation. We will give specific meditations in this book to bring you into more alignment with your guides. It may be necessary to develop a practice of meditation for some time, before your guidance will come to you. It is a commitment to raise your vibration through meditation and letting go of things that no longer serve that will put you on the path to greater closeness to you angel guides. You of course, must be willing to engage in this process but we feel this may be the reason why you picked this book up in the first place. There is a deeper part of you that is seeking this knowledge and knows that it will enhance your life. Allow this to surface and let it guide you to greater engagement with your angels.

Our essence is pure love

Your angels are glad to hear from you and know that you are thinking of them You can pray to them as you would God and they will be willing to help you. They wish you to know that they are not in any way greater than you and they stress that you are their equal. They are here to help you. You are very much equals in a creative partnership together.

How do angels work with those who are unaware or unwilling to admit they exist? They remain present and they hold the person in their intention and send wellbeing toward the person. They are always helping behind the scenes. For example, it could be gently leading the person to people, places or things that can help with their evolution. The level of contact with their angels, depends on the level of the level of resistance from the person. We understand that people are at different stages of openness to this help and communication. We still work to always hold that person in our highest attention. We are always beaming our signal of love towards you. The degree to which you perceive this is the degree to which you are willing to believe it. We, of course, revel in your interaction with us and we want this.

Even if you do not believe in us, we will always hold you in the highest regard and respect and love you without condition anyway. We know that we will be united with you at some stage even if it is not until the day that you leave the earth. On this day too, we will be present with you helping you with your transition to non-physical. At that moment of transition if not before, you will feel the strength and power of our love for you.

Looking outwards at the world currently there seems to be so much turmoil, war and destruction. It is difficult not to be overwhelmed with this tsunami of negativity. We want you to know that while this is happening there is also a great lifting of the collective consciousness. The negativity of the situation is causing many contrary desires for peace and wellbeing. These will become manifest in time. It is important to take personal responsibility for how you are feeling because your negative thoughts can also contribute to the overall consciousness of the world.

Our intention is to let you know the breadth and depth of the love that there is for you on the non-physical plane. We always see you as the greater you, incorporating your higher being. We see you as magnificent creators. The work you do on Earth by living through this time is adding to the whole of creation. The nature of our universe is expansion, and you contribute to the growth through your willingness to be in this life and to co create with the universe. Your life experience is contributing to the expansion of all that is. Therefore, our most prominent feeling for you is that of gratitude and admiration and we continue to beam this towards you. It is important that you are aware of this because we wish that there be no fear at all involved in the process of reaching out to us. We want you to know that though you would try and convince us of your smallness and flaws we could never see anything but your magnificence as the soul you have been over the accumulation of lifetimes you have lived on earth.

CHAPTER 3

Communication with your angels-expanding your personal power

It is our strongest wish and intention that through the writing of this book that you will know that you are not alone. The guides from the angelic realms and your higher being want nothing more than to put you in touch with your inner wisdom and knowing. Life when lived from the perspective of having guides and helpers can be much less onerous. Clarity is the gold that can help you move forward more surely rather than procrastinate or stay stuck.

Audrey, in the Summer of 2019, felt very stuck and was suffering from several physical ailments in addition to mental exhaustion and confusion. She had been on the spiritual path for many years but was not making progress and felt very much mired in the mud. She went to a spiritual healer who helped her clear much of the physical and psychic bonds that had kept her tethered to people places and situations that did not serve her. Almost immediately she noticed that she was feeling lighter. Within a few weeks of this, she woke up one morning at 4am to hearing our voices and began transcribing our guidance daily. We tell you this because many people have this mental and psychic junk that is keeping them stuck and is interfering with them getting in contact with their inner wisdom

It is our intention with this manual to give you easy straightforward ways to cut through and clear this mental clutter that will help you encounter your guides and expand your inner knowing. As a voracious reader of spiritual books Audrey still finds it difficult to integrate the concepts in her own life. She is a highly practical person a characteristic she attributes to her mother's influence. There is a great difference between acknowledging spiritual concepts and making them work for you. There follows in this book, a step-by-step process to become more attuned to your higher being and your spiritual guides. It will take a certain amount of time and commitment to integrate but we know that the rewards will be incredible. Audrey says that the clarity the process of engaging with her guides brings her is like gold to her. The freedom of never having to second guess herself is immense. Audrey thought initially that our guidance would be for the greater state of the planet at this time but was surprised how personal to her that it was. The everyday worries and dilemmas were addressed which gave her the courage of conviction. After years of practice, it came to the place she now feels that almost all her actions are aligned with us and her higher being. "In many ways it has given me back my power" she says. I used to look outside myself for solutions but now I go within. Everything has changed".

Messages from your angels

There are other ways that you can sense us. Many people can use different senses to perceive us and our messages in various ways. We also wish to say we send messages on the lips of others, songs on the radio and in newspapers and magazines. An aware person can spot these and infer their meaning.

It can be very subtle the ways in which we communicate with you. For example, many people find feathers when walking outside in nature. This can be a sign from us which will mean that you are being protected and taken care of. It means in simple terms we are always with you, and you are never alone. It is our wish that you would call on us more for help and assistance.

Another common way is to see lights or colours when you ask to see us in physical form. We will always come to you in a way that is non-threatening to you. We wish to send feedback when asked to show ourselves in physical form. This is why we may manifest in colours for some people while others may not see anything. It depends on the person and what will be meaningful to them also. We wish to communicate in a way that is personal to you but not in any way frightening. When you are in a state of fear you are very much cut off from us and our guidance, so it is always our intention to keep the perceiver feeling safe and at ease.

Audrey hears us when she quietens her mind. This is the easiest way for us to get our message to her. Indeed, she is typing these words as we are speaking to her. For those who can see us we come in forms that are familiar to them and that will mean something to them. We are not male or female, nor do we look human, but we often assume these shapes so our interactions with you will become more meaningful to you. At our basest form we are simply energy.

There are those who can visualise us and this can make the interaction more comprehensive. The shapes we assume may change as time goes by. A few very special individuals will be able to see our truest form or shape. This skill is often with them from childhood. Most children can see us initially in a shape that makes sense to them. In time, most lose this ability as it is trained out of them by their parents or society as not being acceptable. Generally, children are not frightened by this ability to see as they have the understanding that it is normal. Your children are closer to source God because they have more recently been in the non-physical dimension. We urge parents to be curious when their children approach them about seeing spirits or angels. Do not scold them or tell them off. Be open and ask them to describe what they are seeing. If you stay open and unafraid they will be more comfortable. It is also important to emphasise that they are safe and protected.

We have many messengers out in the world also bringing you our messages through YouTube channels, books, seminars and websites and indeed other modalities. Sometimes those people that are on a spiritual path can feel they are constantly hearing the same messages, and this means they are on the right track. Our messages can be across any media because there is no limit to our ability to reach those who are willing to hear. It is often the case that you need to hear something more than once to begin to integrate the message, Audrey finds that she learns best by accessing many different sources. Audiobooks are particularly helpful to her as her primary sense is clairaudience. Also, she learns from podcasts, you tube videos, attending seminars and books.

In summary, it is always out intention to communicate with you in a way that holds most meaning for you. We never wish to frighten or intimidate you in any way. If you would like to connect with us, please know that your intention to do so is that biggest factor in being successful.

Guided Writing and translation of messages

Discernment is important when you perceive messages from your angels. If messages are positive and encouraging, they are more likely to be from your angels or higher being. Any negativity about yourself is mostly coming from your inner critic or from dwelling on other people's opinions of you.

The early morning when you first wake can be a good time to try to receive messages. There are processes we describe later to enhance your ability to get into the vicinity or bandwidth so you can hear your angels. Meditation can be helpful prior to trying to write messages.

Another way to clear your head of any thoughts and emotions to become clear is to allow yourself to free write a few A4 pages of what is going on for you. Get your frustration out on the page and write about anything that is bothering you. This can work by clearing your mental clutter and help you to become more in alignment with your guides.

Begin slowly and allow yourself time. Becoming clear on your intention for the process. For example, if you are hoping to gain clarity and guidance to help you on your souls' path then connecting with the angels is appropriate. Intending that you are given clarity, in whatever way you understand, and for the highest good of all is important. While you may not hear the lesson in your ear, you may be given a life lesson through your life circumstances which brings you to a similar level of knowing. Beginning to trust that the universe and angels have your back is important. Trust that you will be shown the answer you seek, in whatever form you can best receive it.

Audrey sometimes wonders how she is translating our messages to print. She is aware that she has reached a frequency that is adjacent to us so she can hear us. It is indeed more complex than that. We are transmitting a frequency that she then translates into print but there are many more subtle levels to this too, which we would find difficult to explain in words that you would understand. Trust is a huge part of this conversation because if Audrey did not trust us, she would not keep tuning in to us. She also trusts that our guidance will remain with her throughout her life. We did not have to assure here of this, she just assumes it will be there. It is as natural as breathing to her now and her expectation of this also plays a part in the process.

It is most important to know that this guidance is offered to every single one of you without exception. This is something you can have as resource in your own life. The benefits of clarity, reassurance and expanded consciousness will ensue. Your guidance will be delivered in a way that is personal to you and so it can take many forms. We want to assure you of our vast love for you. You are loveable, whole and complete exactly as you are.

Angels and your personal power

It is possible to increase your personal power through the power of intention. You are much more powerful than you can possibly fathom, and your influence goes beyond anything that you can imagine. Even a small gesture of kindness to another can have a profound influence on their life. You cannot always see how it impacts the other person. You can never truly appreciate the full weight of impact you have, but we can. It is like all the little kindnesses light up on a grid. We can see and value all that you do and all that you are. We can often see you more clearly than you can see yourself. We can see your innate goodness even when you have lost track of it yourself. Because we can appreciate the whole of you and all that you do, we truly hold you in high esteem and we beam this vibration back to you always seeing the wellbeing that surrounds you.

Audrey has felt her personal power expand through her communication and interactions with us. This is because she is beginning to move toward believing our assessment of her and it has given her more confidence in herself and her abilities. She can rely on herself to make the best decisions for herself sometimes with the help of our guidance. By using the processes that we will describe later, for example setting intentions, she has realised that she is a co-creator with the universe. These processes have become a part of her life and have led her to believe in herself.

CHAPTER 4

Angel insights to the Law of Attraction

The most compelling reason to be conscious of your thought is to ensure that you create the outcomes that you wish to create in your life. The law of attraction magnifies anything that you give your attention to and so this can work with positive or negative thoughts. You are a magnet for all you attract and in essence you your vibration is the single most important factor in what you attract into your life. Essentially this means you attract more of what you already are. Your mood and your feelings about yourself attract more of the same. Negative thoughts attract negativity while the inverse is true. This works always without exception. Other factors can also influence what you attract into your life. These include expectation, thought forms, entrenched beliefs and previous impactful events such as traumas. This seems to complicate the narrative but really it is very simple you are attracting into your life situations people and things that are in alignment with your vibration and your true feeling on anything at a given time.

Therefore, it is important to ask yourself what your true and deepest feeling on any issue is. For example, you may want to attract large sums of money but deep down you feel money is evil and you are terrified to be corrupted by it. This belief may be a reason why you would then subconsciously repel money because of your fears that it will corrupt you and ruin your life. While the desire for money is real, the underlying feeling here is that money will corrupt so your subconscious rejects money as a way of protection. Beliefs around money are influenced by so many factors such as beliefs inherited from your parents, societal beliefs, ancestral influences, and experiences from this life and past lives. To be aware of the vibration you are transmitting that may or may not attract money, it is necessary to go deep and look at all the layers of belief that you have around the topic. Take an A4 piece of paper and begin to write all the negative thoughts you have about money. You will be amazed what negative beliefs that you were unaware of show up on the page. It is then a good idea to go through each one asking is it true for me. Positive affirmations may help offset negative beliefs around money but only if the belief has been challenged and you have begun to deconstruct it in your mind, so it is no longer true for you. This is time very well spent as it can clear through the mental clutter and negative beliefs that are repelling the money that you strongly desire from coming to you. There are affirmations on abundance in the appendix of this book.

An important thing to note is that the underlying state of mind that you are in when you are wanting anything is what will attract it into your experience. You could say a million affirmations and if you were in a state of feeling not worthy or resentful for example, they would be completely ineffective. The underlying thought or base state of mind is the key. This is because your vibration is the most important factor in what you attract into your life. We wish to affirm the law of attraction as an important law when looking at what manifests in your life. You are a co-creator with the universe and how you feel is important in what you attract into your life.

What does the law of attraction mean for you?

In simple terms it means that what you focus on multiplies. Therefore, if you have a wish, it is important to keep the focus on it and ignore all evidence to the contrary. Your underlying state of being is important when you begin to put your wishes out into the universe. If you find yourself in a dark mood, then that is the time to try and find some positives in your environment to increase your vibration. It is not the time to ask the universe for any new wishes or desires.

We promise that this will be a practical guide to becoming more in tune with the guidance from your angels. There are many steps you can take to become clearer so you can begin to sense and finally hear this guidance. This is available to all of you no exceptions. It is a question of willingness to commit to the steps regularly.

The information we are sending to Audrey to transcribe has not been covered before in such a context. The consciousness of the world is rising in vibration now and things have shifted so that regular people can understand and appreciate the importance of the information we give you here. These conversations have not happened in the past. This is new information that we are downloading from source for this book.

It is our intention with this book to bring you to a higher vibration so you can attract more of what you desire. This book also works through coded messages and imagery to trigger inner knowing in the cells of your body. While the information in this book may be new to you, it is not new to your soul. The purpose of it is to bring a deep remembering to your soul of all the knowledge you have accumulated in your past lifetimes. Your higher being has all the information you have accumulated from all your many past lives. It is true that your higher being knows the secrets of the universe and has much wisdom. The vibration of your higher being is much higher than that of your body which is made up of matter. You can call on the wisdom of your higher being at any time in meditation. It is likely your higher being is constantly sending you messages. By meditating regularly, you can work on developing a connection with your higher being.

Manifesting and the law of attraction.

The state you are in when trying to manifest something is crucial to the outcome. This is not the always the case when intending. When intending it is better to get out ahead of things by intending at the start of the day or during each time you change location in the day. This is because momentum plays a crucial part in the outcome. We always recommend setting intentions early in the day because your mind is clearer and the momentum of your thought has not yet built up. The morning time is the best time to set intentions for the day ahead, use visualisation and really allow yourself to feel what you would like to happen occurring in your mind's eye. The more real you can make it the better.

Meditation is an excellent tool for quietening the mind. It also allows you to communicate with your higher being or I am presence. This can allow you to hear the whisperings of your soul. We recommend you make time to meditate even for fifteen minutes a day. The results can be life changing. Setting intentions after meditation is a good practice and this is a good time to visualise what you would like to occur in the broader scheme of your life.

To be an effective co-creator with the universe it is helpful to know about the law of attraction which means that which is likened to itself is drawn. This means that for example, negativity begets more negativity. The inverse is true of this of this also. The law of attraction is an immutable law of the universe. This is why when you are in a place where negativity is predominant in your vibration it is hard to be positive. It takes incremental steps to get to positivity. Taking a nap can be helpful because it stops all negative momentum.

A key component of this law is momentum. For example, are you on a path that is feeling more positive or is it incrementally getting more negative. It can help to examine the scale as to where you are at in the current moment to move into a better feeling emotion. In a book that Audrey esteems highly, Power versus Force, Dr David R Hawkins describes emotions in terms of vibration with shame being at the lowest vibration while love is at the highest. We all have a vibration that we are operating at. This can be raised and lowered depending on what emotions we are experiencing or our circumstances.

We wish to say that all your emotions are learning devices. They are reflections of how you feel in the moment. The learning comes from how you feel in relation to how you want to feel. As a human being there is a scale of emotions on which you are moving up and down on. It can help to know that every state is temporary and will eventually be replaced by another. There are of course pattens of emotions such as depression when sadness apathy and often shame have led to a prolonged period of these emotions repeating. We wish to say that the inverse of this is also true in that it is possible to live in prolonged periods of bliss. Many of the world's sages and mystics have achieved this state and it available to all humans.

Thinking things into being

We wish to speak about the effect that thoughts have on emotions. It is true that there is a component in the mind concerned with the survival of the organism that alerts the mind to dangers and pitfalls in daily existence. This part, often referred to the ego, is often expanded beyond what is helpful in modern life. It is helpful then to be discerning about the thoughts which are occurring to you. It is a common misperception that you are your thoughts and so you must believe them. We would correct this by saying that you are the perceiver or watcher of your thoughts. Where do these thoughts come from? In order, to explain to you the origin of your thoughts we must go back to explore your makeup as a human on this planet.

Before you agreed to come into your current body you were part of the non-physical universe. When you did come into your current body the greater part of you remained behind in non-physical. This means that you are more than what you can see before you in your physical body. Many people refer to this part that remains in non-physical as your soul. We prefer to refer to it as your higher being. It is the compilation of all you have lived before in all your previous lifetimes. It is all the knowledge and experience and wellbeing and wisdom that you have developed over many past lives and your innate knowledge of the origin and makeup of the universe. It contains the deepest understanding of your place in the universe and on your current and future paths. This higher being is accessible to you. There is a constant signal between you and your higher being. It is constantly holding you in its highest regard. It is beaming you wellbeing from its place in non-physical. It knows exactly what you want and need and the fastest path for you to find it. It holds the akashic records to all your past lives and the culmination of all that wisdom and experience. In short, it is a phenomenal resource that you have at your disposal to help you on your path.

All thoughts have been thought before and are like a bank of stored energy. The thoughts you manage to tap into are largely attracted by your vibration at the time you think the thought. The thought responds to the frequency that you are transmitting out into the world. Very much like turning the nob on the radio to tune into a station. If you are on the same frequency of the thought, it can come to you. Most people will know that they have blocks of thought, where like attracted like, such as bouts of depression. The law of attraction ensures that what is likened to itself is drawn. This is why it can take some time to get the momentum going in the opposite direction especially to negative thought.

Focus... the missing link?

Where you put you focus has very real consequences for the life you create. When you realise this, you can begin chose to focus on thoughts and conditions that bring you joy. The frequency of gratitude and appreciation is very high, and a higher vibration attracts more of the same. Take your attention off the unwanted and focus on the wanted in conjunction with feeling good in the moment and things will change for you. You have the power to do this. It takes a little bit of effort, but you are all well capable of it. In time it becomes easier to focus on the wanted.

If you want to be wealthy do not give attention to the lack of funds in your bank account. Focus on what it would feel like, look like, taste like and smell like to be wealthy. If you want a body that is different from your current shape do not focus on your current shape rather what your new body would feel like in terms of energy and enjoyment and appearance.

If you are lonely and have few friends, do not focus on the lack of friends rather the characteristics of the new friends you want to attract into your life. If you do not have a partner and would like one, take you attention off the lack and focus on the characteristics of a life partner that appeal to you.

If your children are irritating you because they are always fighting, take your attention off the fighting and place it on the aspects of your children that you appreciate. Better still write a list. This will allow a shift to take place in the relationship when you are appreciating your children for the individuals they are.

Of course, many point out that focusing on the wanted is

ignoring reality. It can seem like we are asking you to gaslight yourself. We are not. If your reality is negative, it is ok to acknowledge and accept this but then take your attention off it to avoid more negativity being drawn to the situation. When focusing on the negative not only does it not help you by lowering your vibration, it is feeding negativity into the collective unconscious also. When you stop the negative thought by appreciating anything small that pleases you, you stop the negative momentum and allow the law of attraction to bring you positive thoughts.

Often when trying to bring about a condition in your life you will put your focus into thoughts and feelings that make you feel positive about the outcome. If something is a long-held desire, then you must turn your focus on it frequently for change to occur. It is not sufficient to just imagine it once; it needs to be kept active in your focus daily or as regularly as possible.

CHAPTER 5

Intention - Increasing your personal powers of attraction

We cannot overstate the value of intention. Intention is just focusing your mind on what you want to happen in your life. You can write down or intend it in your mind. It is useful when starting a new project to ask yourself what your intention for it is. Intention setting daily or an hour-by-hour basis is an excellent way of letting the universe know exactly what you would like to show up in your experience. You cannot overuse this. It remains powerful no matter what the situation.

Audrey does not always remember to intend every day. On the days she works she does always do so in her car on the way there. She intends ease, focus, harmony and enjoyment before she goes into her workplace. Frequently her work runs smoothly and easily. She almost never runs into complications and her relationship with her work colleagues is excellent. She sets an intention for safety frequently while travelling in her car. By setting intentions for yourself on a regular basis you begin to come to the realisation that you are in fact a co-creator with the universe of your experience. You gradually begin to become more empowered. You realise you don't have to just sit back and let your life happen to you. You can take control, and you can be an active participant in how your life turns out.

Intention is a very powerful way to hack what happens to you daily and influence the course of your life. It is so simple. It is just a matter of saying to yourself or writing down what you want to happen in the day. It is important not to leave these things to chance use intention to help you get what you want. You can change the intentions as you are progressing through different parts of your day. For example, you may intend safety and flow of traffic when you first get into your vehicle at the start of the day. If you are heading to an important meeting, you can intend harmony and ease before going in. Also, this can be used before you go on the phone to a person. It helps focus your mind as to what is most important to you on any given day. After a while it becomes a habit and becomes easier to do.

Intention is a superpower you never knew you had. It is important to know that you are a powerful creator of all that has occurred and will occur in your life. This can be a hard concept to initially accept because of course there are things that have happened in your life that you would not have wished to occur. Nonetheless, it is a basic law of the universe that you create your life circumstances from your thoughts. In truth, you co-create with the universe which is based on the law of attraction. You must never blame yourself for things that are undesirable that have happened in your life. In another part of the equation humans often have karma from past lives that may play out in this life. Also, there are experiences that souls agree to before reincarnating on earth so there is a little more nuance to the creation of reality. However, your thoughts and expectations remain a very strong component in what you manifest. The very good news about this is that you can adjust these variables accordingly with very powerful results.

Intention can be used for greater periods of time. Intentions can be set at the start of the year. When starting a new projection setting an intention can be a very important. You can bring intention into parenting for example always holding the intention that decisions you make will be for the highest wellbeing of your child. Setting intentions brings you clarity as to what you want to achieve in any circumstance, and this multiplies your power in attracting it to you. By setting intentions you are also telling the universe that you believe in your ability to attract your wishes. This shift to expectation from passive resignation is also very powerful in helping you attract what you want.

We can't overstate the benefits of intention. It pre paves the path for you and focuses your mind on what you want to attract out of any situation. You are using your power as a co-creator of your life when you use the power of intention. It immediately shifts you from a person adrift in a sea of coincidences and accidents. It challenges the view that life is happening to you, and you have no control of events. We would say life is happening for you and you are indeed a co-creator of all that happens to you. You co create with the universe or source. Instantly the belief that you are a creator places you in a position of power. You are no longer helplessly waiting for life to happen to you. You are instead focusing on what you want to happen and putting out your intentions. Every prayer is heard and is granted at the time of asking but the timeline of when this materialises into matter for you, depends on several factors. We will talk more about manifestation of wishes further along in this book.

We would like to clarify how intending something is different to praying. When you pray for another, it is connecting with the divine for the purposes of moving positive energy towards the person or place. It is an energy transfer, and it is felt, and it is effective and powerful. Intention varies in that it involves putting some energy into achieving the outcome of your desire. Previsualising and focusing on what outcome you desire energises it and is aligned with the law of attraction. As focus is a currency and is valuable and as visualisation also adds power it stacks the odds in your favour.

Setting intensions daily or more frequently can be hugely helpful in living your life in a more joyful way. When you start this process, it can be interesting to sit back and see what results. For example, before making an important phone call it can be helpful to set the intention around what you would like to occur. Possible intentions could be ease of communication and harmony or for the other person to be able to hear what you are saying. Audrey has seen this in her own life when dealing with individuals that others would describe as difficult. She has found setting an intention for harmony and ease of communication has been very helpful. Often the person with whom she is interacting reacts graciously towards her or at the very least remains courteous. These so-called difficult people are different with her because she has set an intention, and it has made a difference to how the interaction has unfolded.

Your focus influences what you attract

We would say you can't intend too often or overuse this tool. To set an intention it is important to be fully conscious and aware when doing so. Your scientists have found that bringing your awareness or attention to something changes the outcome, that is, observing a phenomenon changes it.

Quantum mechanics is the study of how particles at the atomic and subatomic level interact with each other and their environment. The observer effect is the phenomenon in which the act of observation alters the behaviour of the particles being observed. This effect is due to the wave-like nature of matter, which means that particles can exist in multiple states simultaneously. When an observer measures a particular property of a particle, they are effectively collapsing the wave-function of that particle, causing it to assume a definite state.

This is the power of bringing attention to something. In order, to set an intention, you must bring your attention to the present moment. All power exists in the present moment and never in the past or future. You come into the present moment to take stock of everything and to decide what you would like to create in your life going forward. This simple action harnesses your power in the moment which is the only place your power is.

An intention works because you are present. You have brought your conscious awareness to the situation, and you have decided how or what you would like to create in the future. It is your attention to the moment that is the powerful aspect. Your attention in the moment or your presence or conscious awareness is the vital element in the process of creation or co- creation with the universe. The results of what you set out to manifest are proportional to the quality of your focus or conscious awareness at the time the intention is being set. This means a pure and present awareness is very powerful compared to the split energies of for example a distracted person.

Another element that has been largely overlooked is the frequency at which intentions are set. Many people feel that it is sufficient to set an intention or ask the universe for something once. We say that the magnitude of the intentions can be greatly amplified through frequent repetition of these intentions. This can be done through setting intentions while you are moving through your day. It can also be achieved by writing down intentions which also adds power to them. Saying them out loud or sharing them with others does not always amplify your intentions. The nuance here is knowing when to share and if these ideas are not fully developed then it may be best to keep them within yourself to allow the momentum to build before sharing them externally.

The morning can be a good time to set intentions because the momentum of the day has not yet set in. This is especially pertinent when it comes to the momentum of your thoughts. Many people wake up and almost immediately a barrage of negative thoughts can assail them. Meditation and setting intentions first thing in the morning can be helpful before the momentum of other thoughts take over. We would recommend meditation first followed by intention setting for the day. This can help you get the day off on a good footing.

Visualising the outcome of intentions

Be specific when setting intentions. It can be helpful if you are a visual person to visualize how you would like the day to unfold. Picture the places you will go and the interactions you would like to have with other people. Playing things out in your head before they happen can be a powerful way to intend if you are a visual person. We all have experienced the power of this creating for example, picturing something that you dread happening in minute detail and feeling it viscerally only for it to manifest later in the day. This is a very effective way to create as most of you can attest to. It therefore so helpful to flip the negative idea for the positive one and to visualise what you want to experience in as much detail as you can to amplify the power of the intention.

Adding in all the senses when setting intentions or visualising how you would like your day to go is very important. How will you feel when this event is taking place? What can you see and hear, taste or touch? What does the overall picture look like? Make it so real in your mind's eye that you would have difficulty knowing whether it is reality or fantasy. The more real you can make it, the more power it has behind it the more likely you are to have or live that experience.

The mind has trouble deciphering fantasy from reality and so the feeling of having something that you desire manifest for you can be very important in the process. The feeling like it is already done and what it would be like to have can amplify by hundreds the power to attract what you desire. It has been accepted by many and forms the basis of many books on manifestation. We want to tell you know how and why it works so you can appreciate its importance and moreover be able to apply it to your own life successfully.

This works when the fantasy of what you would like to manifest is compelling by using visualisation and all the other senses your body and mind believe that it has already happened. There is no resistance in the mind or body. As mentioned, resistance can be formed by your belief system and what you expect to happen. By focusing on the fantasy until it is compelling in your mind you have hacked the brain and body into believing it has already occurred. The compelling nature of the fantasy amplifies your desire and intention to bring about this scenario. Therefore, the formula of amplified desire in the presence of reduced or negligent resistance must ensure that the desire is brought about.

Amplifying Variables

Further amplifying variables can be strength of desire, allowing the sensations of the fantasy becoming reality and willingness to linger with the good feelings around the desire. Time in of itself is not of any consequence in this unfolding process however the person must be prepared to spend some time on the process. The power of intention or desire amplifies when given intention and focus. It does not have to be a long period of time. Even a few minutes can be effective if you are thoroughly focused and engaged. Time spent amplifying desires and setting intentions is always time well spent as it is a major factor in the process of manifestation.

When it comes to personal power it is important to examine the ways you may have given it away to others and to life situations. It is true that society, through a drip feed of negative news stories, can contribute greatly to a climate of fear. When acting from a place of fear you are not accessing your true power. Most humans have also been negatively programmed in childhood to see their limitations rather than their talents and the massive potential that they hold. There are also many personal beliefs that you hold that are limiting your life choices and your expectation of what you may be do or have. It makes sense to examine these and try and rid yourself of them. A belief is simply a thought that you keep thinking, it doesn't have to have any hold over you, if you don't give it any of your power.

Most of you have had incidences as children where your power was diminished through the actions of others be it parents or teachers. Those others felt that they had to point out your limitations to help you. This played out in events that have influenced your outlook and expectations for a very long time or for many until they die. Now is the time to take these perceived limitations out and really question them. If they are the opinion of another person, they can have no effect on you if you withdraw any power from them. The people that acted in this way were acting out of a sense of fear or scarcity thinking. Their perceptions and ideas do not need to have any power over you if you don't allow them to.

It is a helpful way to examine those perceptions of your own that may be out of alignment. Realising that your thoughts are often not true and that they are keeping your stuck is often the first step to becoming happier. Negative thought can lead to negative emotion and that can impact on what you manifest in your life. Question your thoughts and tell yourself a positive story to see change in your life.

CHAPTER 6

Self Love, your highest intention

We wish to speak about this now because there is an epidemic of self -loathing and self-blame in the world and it leading to untold misery and distress. The feelings that you have about yourself when you are in this state could not be further from how we see you as a magnificent creator and beautiful being of love. This inner dialogue seems to be very common to almost every one of you and we notice that how you speak to yourself is often not kind. There is a harshness that persists within many of you, when it comes to the self. Most would not speak to a friend the speak internally to themselves.

Through conditioning from a young age, you have allowed the opinions of others to be more predominant that your own feelings of worth and power. It was a gradual process and one that was difficult to avoid in your current environment. The connection you sought with those around you to survive made you adopt behaviours to ensure you were part of the group. These behaviours such as people pleasing and putting others before yourself were necessary at the time.

The good news is that your natural state is one of appreciation of self. When you first came in as a new baby you knew that you were inherently worthy and deserving. You proceeded to complain when your needs were not met. You loved every part of yourself then and that was your nature. You knew you were deserving of love and having all your needs met. In time, you developed coping mechanisms within your families to keep you safe. You began to place others' opinions of you above your own and in that way, you devolved your power to them. The world around you at the time was also sending you messages about what you deserved. For example, in relation to what you owned, how you looked and who you were friends with.

We wish to say you are deserving at the very core of your being, and you do not need to do anything to change yourself. You deserving just as you are. You are loved just as you. We refer you to the meditation on feeling the love that the angels have for you. If you were aware of even a fraction of the love that we have for you, the force of it would bring you to your knees. We have so much love for you.

The question then is how can you come to love yourself? We can give you some processes that can help but it will take some time because of the momentum you may have going on self-judgement. As always, setting an intention to be loving and kind to yourself is important. Write this down and keep it where you can see it daily. If you can begin to catch yourself when you begin to have unloving thoughts. You don't have to counteract them but saying this is just a story I am telling myself can be helpful. Be kind to yourself at times when there is strong momentum going towards the unworthy and disparaging self-talk. It will take time for this to gradually become less of a habit. If you can practice the self-love meditation and practice sending loving energy to yourself regularly this can help. It is safe to release what is not serving you and put boundaries in place.

Setting boundaries to preserve your energy.

Putting boundaries in place when it comes to your life is a sign of someone that loves themselves. This action tells the world that your time and energy are important. It is an act of radical power to put boundaries in place because it honours you first and foremost. People who have good boundaries have less burn out because they do not over stretch themselves. They also have less resentment because the person who is doing it all and helping everyone and always putting themselves last is carrying resentment. This is almost always the case. You can see it when these people who are martyrs for others suddenly erupt with anger seemingly out of the blue, but this had been building up because of all the self- sacrifice that was finally intolerable.

Can you start today to put some boundaries in place that respect your energy and time. It can take time and effort, but it is so worth it. It is our promise that you can create a life that you love but you must start putting yourself first and have some boundaries. Having a boundary says to the world I respect myself and I value my time. It says that I esteem myself and I stay true to my values and instincts. It says I care about how I feel as I know it is key to manifesting the life I want and so I am going to focus on things that make me, and my body feel good. It may take time and effort but every time you put a boundary in place you are taking back some of your energy. There is a process later in the book called the energetic map. By completing this you will be aware of all the places your energy is flowing and decide where you want to direct your energy.

An example of a boundary is that you may decide that you no longer will tolerate people being deliberately disrespectful to you. Audrey once ended a conversation with a person who became abusive on the phone. She ended it with the line. “I never let anybody speak to me like that”. She has continued in this vein and has followed up when others were disrespectful with the person directly and on other occasions with the organisation they represented. She would say that for many years she was unable to do this and put others' needs ahead of her own. For Audrey this has been a part of taking her power back and she has never regretted speaking up for herself.

Another way to become more loving towards yourself is to write down at least ten things you love to do. Ask yourself if it is possible to include one or two of those things in your week. Most people will find excuses for why they can't do this, arguing that they don't have time or that it is selfish. We say it is essential to plan for this time for yourself, because when you act in the direction of things you love to do, the universe supports you and will put more of those things on your path. Your life will begin to feel more expansive and to have more possibilities when you give yourself time to do what you love. For those of you that are parents this has a payoff too because you are a better parent when you have taken some time and resourced yourself. In essence everybody gains.

This can apply to the bigger desires in your life such as changing jobs or attracting abundance. The more time and space you can give yourself to work out what you want will help move you in the direction in which you want to go. To those of you that are feeling stuck, even one small action can make a big difference in your life whether it is taking a short walk or deciding to drink more water. It is the little cumulative actions that move you in the direction you want to go. We know that you can take small steps to prioritise yourself and begin to move towards a more rewarding life right now. Take one step today that moves you in the direction of a more fulfilling life.

Self-love and compassion towards the self are so important for healthy self-esteem. You will make mistakes in your life and being able to forgive yourself is essential. Often it can be easy to offer compassion to another for the mistakes that they make. You are often loving and forgiving towards others but don't give yourself the same grace. We say do this, make peace with the past and allow yourself this grace.

We include some questions here as they are pertinent to the theme of self-love.

I have difficulty accepting myself as I am. Can you help me with self-acceptance?

Self-acceptance is a process. Many of you have become so conditioned by others' opinions of you that you have forgotten that you have the power to give acceptance and love to yourself. This is the purest form of love for without it all relationships serve only the ego and are formed from a sense of lack.

The process of writing positive aspects of the self can be very powerful. Try to add to the list or at least look at the list every day. The aim of this is to come to the realisation that you are a person who has made mistakes, and you are worthy of receiving compassion. Self-compassion is very powerful, and it has the power to change completely how you feel about yourself. Becoming still and feeling into your heart space you can expand the love in your heart and extend it to any part of your body.

It is important to watch for negative self-talk and blaming which most of you indulge in, to a lesser or greater extent. When you find yourself berating yourself just come back into your body, take a few deep breaths and offer compassion to yourself as described above. Saying things like I am doing my best and everything is working out for me can be stabilising and counteract the negative self-talk. Again, it is important to realise that this will take time, but the power is in catching the negative self-talk because you have become conscious to have achieved this. Every time you can do this it is a mini victory.

How can I have more faith in myself?

It may be helpful to come to the viewpoint that we have of you. We see you as your whole self-incorporating your higher being who has many lifetimes behind it. The wisdom of this higher being and the aliveness and energy of your soul is what we gauge when we see you. To see is even a misnomer because we have more senses than the conventional ones you have of sight, touch, hearing, smell and taste. If we were to describe it, it would be more like a feeling of your energy blueprint. Your soul has a record of all past lifetimes, and it is called your akashic record. We see this too when we sense you. The enormity of your whole self is something to behold. You really are quite amazing. We are in awe of you. If you could even for a moment see the beautiful brilliance that the whole of you encompasses you would never doubt yourself again.

We know it seems like a big ask but could you even for a minute try to image the totality of your being. It is not possible to see what we see from the physical plane because of the difference in vibration between the two planes. Could you begin to allow the possibility of the power that is the whole of you? Is there any way you can begin to sense the truth of these words? The best way is to pause and ask how does this information make you feel? Is there anything in your body responding to it? Do not worry if this is not the case, sit with it and allow it to titrate.

So, you see that we have a very expansive view, and we see you in your totality as the powerful creator that you are. How does this line up with how you see yourself? We see that most here are acutely aware of their perceived limitations, while not being fully aware of the great power and potential that they have. This is not something we can teach you with words. When getting to the truth of things, your feelings will guide you best. Does it seem possible that you have hidden potential and that you are more powerful than you have been led to believe? We say being led because most of you have been led to believe in your limitations by your upbringing and by societal messaging. Other people's perceptions of you are not your business but you have let them dictate how you see yourself and the world. In truth this is difficult to avoid due to your conditioning as a small child. There is no blame attached to this. However, now can you sense that there are other possibilities and paths ahead for you? We say there as many as you believe there to be.

Belief in the self can be achieved in small incremental actions. It can be as simple as beginning to countenance that there could be a different future ahead for you. It could be taking you attention off that stressful thought that tells you that you are not good enough. It could be allowing yourself to daydream alternative realities. It could be journaling in the morning to help you recognise how you feel about something or doing something that makes you feel good in your body. It can be taking time for a walk on your own in the woods. It could be just being gentle with yourself and allowing yourself to rest if you are feeling tired.

You cannot possibly know all the positive impacts you have had on other people throughout your lifetimes and what the repercussions of these have been. A smile at a person you are crossing paths with. Holding the door open for someone. A text message to someone you know is going through a hard time. All these ways that you shine your light in the world are hugely impactful. You cannot possibly know the knock-on effect of these small positive actions, but we do. The smallest gesture can have the biggest impact on someone's life. These gestures can and have saved lives. So, you see, the small things are not in fact small after all.

We want to say that you have been measuring your worth wrongly all along. You are not the contents of your bank account, the title of your job, your role in your family and especially not what others perceive you to be. You are a spiritual being having a human experience and the bigger part of you remains in non-physical retaining all the knowledge and wisdom of past lives and a much broader view of the universe and all of creation.

I am always stopping myself from doing things I would enjoy because I put others first or want to be perceived as putting others first. How can I allow myself to put myself first.

We would say it is not selfish to put yourself first. We have mentioned this before, and we feel it is helpful to be somewhat selfish. You cannot help others if your own well has run dry from lack of self-care and attention. You came to this planet knowing that you would be a creator in the moment having experiences that cause you to desire certain conditions and watching these desires coming to fruition. It is a dynamic process of manifestation. It is impossible to manifest the life you desire when you put others needs ahead of yourself constantly. Of course, it is fine to help others as much as you can and indeed, we do realize that those of you with children do quite rightly prioritise their wellbeing. That is not to say that you should be a martyr that always puts others first as this serves nobody especially not you and ultimately leads to resentment. Balance in this as in all things is important.

We feel that other peoples' opinions of you are their own business. Therefore, acting based on the perception of others and their opinions is in plain terms not serving yourself. Take time to be still and contemplate what you really desire and allow yourself to have some of what you desire. This will help you rise your vibration and will have the knock-on effect of uplifting others around you in your circle.

Self-compassion meditation

Having love and compassion for yourself can be the start of your healing journey. When you are at war with yourself through self-criticism and self-judgement you are splitting your energy. You are building up resistance to accepting yourself just as you are which is the key to your peace of mind. If you have compassion for yourself, it frees you up to see that you are just doing your best in the world and that you appreciate yourself.

- Go somewhere quiet where you won't be disturbed. Sit upright or lie down. Bring your attention to your breath. Allow your breathing to deepen with your exhalations longer than your inhalations. Remain for 2 mins just focusing on your breathing,
- Place your left hand on your heart and your right hand on your belly. Feel your heart beating beneath your hand. Place you attention into your heart space. Visualise a pink disc of energy rotating very fast. This is your heart chakra. Allow this energy to expand
- Think about all the love you have in your heart. Expand and multiply this energy until you can feel it as a surge of energy.
- Allow the pink light to radiate out into your body. If you have an area of your body that needs healing, you can direct the energy there. Allow your body to be bathed in this beautiful pink light
- Say the following

I am loving and my heart is filled with love and compassion. I allow myself to feel the love in my heart. My capacity for love and compassion is infinite. I now extend this love and compassion to myself and my body. I love and accept myself as I am.

- Take a few minutes to sit in the energy and allow it to settle.

Affirmations for Self-love

I love and accept myself exactly as I am right now.
I appreciate all that I am.
I allow myself to feel loving towards myself.
I now see all the ways I uplift others.
I am whole and complete exactly as I am
I am loving towards myself in my thoughts and words.
I allow myself to receive love from others.
I deserve to be loved and appreciated just because I exist.

Say these affirmations to become more loving and appreciating of yourself. They can be said aloud or silently. If one resonated with you, place it in a prominent position where it can be seen and repeated daily.

We end this section with a channelled section from Audrey's guides.

Dearest one, you are beloved
We adore you and hold you in the highest esteem.
Your magnificence is astounding to us.
You are the brightest shiniest star in the sky.
Your depth is greater than the ocean,
Your potential and power are limitless.
You are deserving of the greatest joy and abundance.
You are deserving of everything your world can offer you.
You are deserving because you exist right now.
You are deserving just as you are.
If only you could fathom a small amount of the light you carry.
It would be blinding to your eyes.
Please believe us when we say you are a powerful being and you have the potential to have a life that is exactly as your desire it to be.

You are beloved here on the non-physical plane. There are countless who adore you.
We honour you and send you love and blessings.
The love we have for you is boundless.
Beloved one, step into the light of your being and stand in your power.

CHAPTER 7

Clearing the clutter, the first step

The mental clutter that the average person carries around with them can be a great impediment to connecting to us. This modern lifestyle has become increasingly busy. It seems to many that everything is speeding up, and the pace of life seems to have kicked up a gear. The messages that are transmitted subliminally from advertising is that you are somehow lacking and can only be made whole by buying their merchandise. This is a self-serving agenda by industry. The truth is you are already whole and complete. You also have everything you need to become more centred, whole and in touch with us. There is nothing outside you required. In truth you must go within. It is the only way to foster a connection with your angels but also to increase the peace and contentment that you feel.

The continuous cycle of bad news and catastrophe from the media ensure that the general population are kept in a perpetual state of fear and foreboding. It does not serve the individual, rather it does serve those who wish to keep you from stepping into your power. We wish you to take your intention off these factors by exposing yourself to them less, for example not watching the news. Withdraw your attention from it so you can create a reality that serves your higher purpose. When you are emotionally triggered by bad news it lowers your vibration and that has a direct effect on what you manifest or receive in your life. It does not serve you to become emotionally involved in the bad news stories of the world. When your vibration lowers you cannot act in that moment to help another. You are stuck in that vibration of helplessness and despair. The way to help is by caring about your vibration and how you feel as this ensures that you act from a place of power. When you are centred you also take aligned action which is infinitely more powerful. Here are some tips

- Do not watch or listen to the mainstream news.
- Withdraw your attention from dialogues relating to problems in the world. Be polite and withdraw knowing that staying will not uplift either of you.
- Do not speak about what you do not want to manifest. An example might be if you are sick that you ring all your friends to let them know that you are unwell adding momentum to the illness. Be easy in your thoughts about it knowing that it is working its way through your body and that you will soon be well.
- Care about how you feel and be aware of factors which may bring your vibration down such as negative conversations, people or places.
- Be aware that you can have a great deal of control over your vibration if you are aware of what influence you are under and act accordingly to preserve your highest vibration possible.
- Clarity can be yours when you intentionally set out to clear the mental, psychic and metaphysical clutter from your life.

A wonderful way to help to release mental clutter is free writing, or journaling. For this to work well you need to give yourself some time, such as 15- 20 minutes to allow what needs to arise to arise. This is different to journalling with the angels to receive messages. Instead, the intention should be to let go of what is troubling you. Even if you don't know this at a conscious level it will find its way onto the page. It can help you work your way through emotions. Audrey has sometimes been so angry that she wrote the word on every line for 3 foolscap pages. At the end of this her anger had dissipated to some degree or she had some idea how to proceed. Free writing has helped Audrey clear the mental clutter when it comes to being creative because it processed the thoughts and emotions that were obscuring her ideas and creative impulses.

We urge you to give this a chance. Many would say they have no time but would spend longer aimlessly scrolling on their phone. By making time and space for this during the day even a few times a week, you are giving yourself a sounding board that gives you space and allows you feel what emotions are coming up for you. It is our assertion that it helps to process your emotions too to a certain degree. By giving yourself this time and space then you are also telling the universe that you are worthy of space and time. It is our promise that you will experience positive change in your life and attract new and expansive opportunities also.

Clearing the Clutter- Physically

The first thing to consider is the space you are living in. It is cathartic to remove the physical clutter in your environment. Energetically speaking it also allows you to welcome new things into your life. This is a key principle of the art of Fung shui. Clearing the rubbish from the space is important but also to clear away clothes and items that you are not using is some important. Adding more colour to walls and having plants and flowers around you can be helpful in lifting your vibration. Your environment does profoundly affect your state of mind and vibration.

Clearing your energetic body

It is possible to intentionally or unintentionally take on the burdens worries and energies of others. Energetically you can pick up some negative energies from others either in your aura and physical body. Your aura is the energetic forcefield around your body. Some people are so open they take on more. It is always a good idea to ground and clear your energy regularly.

-If possible, go outside and stand barefoot on the Earth. You can send any heavy energy from your body and auric field down into the Earth for transmutation. It can be indoors, and you can visualise this energy being sent down into the earth.

-You can visualise positive energy flowing up from the base of your feet up through your body and filling all the spaces the energy left. The earth has a blue green energy so you can visualise that colour. Alternatively, you can ask your angels to send pure white light down into your crown chakra and allow this to fill all the spaces where energy was released.

It can be helpful to set boundaries when dealing with negative people. Being mindful of where your physical energy is flowing is crucial. There is a mapping exercise later in the book, which is helpful for becoming more aware where your energy is flowing.

Clearing the clutter emotionally

The most effective way to do this is to become more aware of your emotions and set an intention to feel them as they are occurring. It takes a huge amount of energy to repress your emotions, and this can be draining. Allowing emotions to come up and feel them can be the start of freeing up this energy. It can be uncomfortable to feel your emotions but if you stay present with the physical sensations in your body even if it manifests as pain, you will begin to see that they will shift and dissipate. By doing this more often you learn to be less afraid of your emotions. Your body graciously protects you from intense emotional pain in many ways, but this can take a toll. Be open and curious to exploring your emotions and allowing them to move through you.

Clearing your soul energy.

You can set an intention to clear this energy too. Ask the angels to help you with this as you won't understand the extent of the clearing your soul needs as you are not privy to your past lives.

It can be helpful to work with a healer on this one. Many people see healers for past life regression and other energetic treatments. The angels will work with you on this if you ask for their help.

A more detailed process to become grounded and clear energy.

This is an important to do regularly. It is important that you can clear your energy because you can often take imprints from places and people you have been with and so protection comes into play there. This does not all have to be negative. Often this can be positive like feeling good after meeting an uplifting friend.

Grounding into the earth and sending any negative or heavy energies downwards can be helpful in clearing your energetic field. Walking barefoot on the Earth naturally does this. Use you intention to send this energy downwards. Audrey likes the below process for grounding.

Visualise a ball between your feet and a cord attaching to the ball from your trunk. You can also kneel to do this process. You are going to send this ball deep down into the earth. You now send negative energy down along the cord to the ball in the earth. Visualize energy releasing from your auric field or the field around your body and send this down. Allow 20 to 30 seconds to pass while the energy is moving. You are now ready to receive energy back from mother earth. Visualise beautiful blue energy flowing back up from the Earth filling all the spaces from the clearing. Visualise it radiating out into your auric field. Allow a minute to bathe in this beautiful energy. Now disconnect from the cord. It can be helpful to call on Archangel Michael to seal any points that were opened while the energy was flowing. (Pathway Teaching)

Now you have grounded and cleared your energy you can now protect yourself. It is always important to ground and clear before asking for protection. Archangel Michael is the angel to call on for protection. Close your eyes and call him in. You should feel a shift in energy; some people can visualise him or his colours usually a light blue. Call him three times and wait. Once you feel any shift you can ask him to put you in a golden bubble of light for protection. When finished, thank him and release him until the next time you work with him.

The processes above of clearing physically emotionally and energetically can have a profound effect on your life and energy. The more often that you can do these processes the more benefit you will accrue.

CHAPTER 8

A Blueprint to connection-Steps to tuning into your angelic guidance

These are important aspects when it comes to opening a clearer path to being able to hear guidance. Many of them require deep work that may take a lifetime to achieve, and so for that reason are not a prerequisite to connection. These are just some ideas to put you in our vicinity more than anything else. These are not lofty ideals; they very much relate to where you are as a human right now and contain universal truths as we see them.

1-Faith

It is difficult to know what faith is. In this case we describe it as merely acknowledging the possibility that we exist. Even leaving the door slightly ajar can allow us to impact your life and connect with you. It may be a new concept but is there any part of it that would make sense or feel right to you if you investigated your feelings? Does anything feel familiar? What is your gut telling you? If you can ponder these questions and perhaps leave a small opening for us to enter your life more fully if you see fit.

2-Cultivating silence

Is it possible to find a space in your day when you connect in with yourself. Focusing on your breathing can be helpful and has been proven to relax the nervous system. Just bringing your attention into the body can have the effect of calming you down. Taking quiet time at any stage of your day can allow you time to decompress and feel your feelings. Allow yourself to feel how you feel and let the feelings come through you. They will pass and your energy will have changed.

3-Meditation

We see meditation as a stopping of resistance and an allowing of moments of space so that clarity can begin to flow to you. It can be good to meditate in the morning as a way of getting yourself out ahead of the day. The momentum of thought has stopped when you are asleep, and it can be a good time to tune in for this reason. If you can dedicate even 10 to 20 minutes to it at this time it can be very helpful. Of course, it is a learned skill, and it can take time before your thoughts can slow to where you can begin to get a sense of space. If you can take an approach of curiosity to what arises and allow any thoughts to pass through without becoming attached to them. It will get easier in time. There are meditations in this book that will bring you through the process.

4-Accepting the place where you now are

This is important because it releases all resistance by stopping fighting against what is. The momentum of the problem is halted when you accept where you are at because you are not placing resistance on your path by striving against. Accepting where you are, can be one of the hardest, most radical things to do and it takes bravery. This is because your mind wants to convince you that by accepting whatever circumstance you are in, you are giving up. This is not true; you are simply deciding not to struggle against the current moment. Two things will happen; one is that you release all the negativity about the situation. Second you come into the present moment where your power is and in alignment with your higher being. All decisions made from this place are aligned and much more likely to be successful. Acceptance is the path of least resistance. In your life can you ask yourself what is the path of least resistance? Are there things that you can let go of that no longer serve you? Can you give yourself permission to put your wellbeing above pleasing others? By letting go of something that is not serving you, you can make space for something new and exciting. Perhaps there are some things that you can release that would be easy wins right now. You will know what these are, trust yourself.

5-Facing life's traumas.

We realise this is a momentous task and really is a life's work. It is a balance because for momentum to take place in the direction of joy it is important to focus on joyful and positive thoughts. This is where we differ from other angelic teachers who would be in favour of spiritually bypassing. There can be an excessive pressure to focus on positive thoughts to the detriment of facing actual life events that have been traumatic and integrating them into your life. There may be clarity in looking back on it and how it has impacted you in your current life situation. This is very difficult, and we acknowledge most will need some sort of support with this.

A key point is that the body can hold on to these memories, and the body may need to process them on a physical level also.

This can seem frightening, and it can be difficult, but most traumas need healing on a physical, mental and soul level.

Your inner child may hold the information for you about your past experiences. It can be beneficial to journal to connect to that part of you. It is possible to do this through meditation also. Often people can have a reactive part of themselves that relates back to experiences as a child. When these issues are acknowledged, it can help them to move forward. Often this part needs assurance and you can direct love and compassion towards it.

This is a balance and of course dwelling on these issues without any release can be detrimental too. Also prolonged discussion and dissecting may not always be helpful as it ensures that the negative thoughts lead to a lowering of vibration. The balancing of light and darkness can be helpful. Not staying too long on anything that is distressing and trying to find light moments in every day. We believe it is better to acknowledge and seek help for your life's traumas so you can integrate it in your life.

As a side note we say that when reincarnating into this current life you broadly knew what the contrasting episodes of your life would be. So, from a metaphysical point of view, you were aware. This not to apportion any blame just to say that perhaps there may be strengths you have developed or insights that can be gleaned from these distressing experiences. It is ok if you are not at a stage to come to these conclusions. This may come at another stage or not at all. You cannot possibly know why these experiences occurred or what part they played in your soul contract or life's purpose. We are seeing it from a higher level can. Experiences of contrast cause growth and expansion and we can see the worth of them even if that is difficult from a human perspective. They contribute to the expansion of the whole of your being and to the expansion of the whole of the universe.

6-Letting go

There is no prerequisite needed before connecting with us. The points in this blueprint are suggestions that may help you become clearer and more open to our guidance. Perhaps there is something that is consuming your thoughts and energy and that you would like to let go of. You will know when the time is right. Are you willing to release a little part of it or the whole of it?

Perhaps for example, you may be angry at a friend, resentment may be taking over your thoughts, and you may be obsessed with getting revenge. In this scenario it is you who is suffering and not your friend who even if he knows you are annoyed, has no idea of your mental turmoil. You are poisoning your mind with thoughts that have no effect on your friend, it is something that you are doing to yourself. The good news is you can begin to let it go. Can you release a small part of it for example when the thoughts come up, distracting yourself from getting sucked into spiralling thoughts about the situation. Knowing that it is for your benefit you could say, I am willing to let go of this grudge. This willingness is enough, and you may be often able to feel a shift in energy. It is best not to lie if you are not willing, better to take it slow and when the thoughts arise distract or affirm, I am not going to think about this now. Give yourself a little space and see what arises.

Letting go through intention or being willing to release negative thought and situations is very powerful. Letting go can allow new energy to flow into your life and it can facilitate change. You can take energetic letting go to your surroundings and let go of possessions and things that no longer serve you. By releasing the old you can make room for the new.

A simple statement such as I am willing to let go of the resentment about (whatever applies) is very helpful. It doesn't mean you have to do it straight away but by being willing you can release it piece by piece.

7-Affirmations

Affirmations have become popular in the last few years, and this has been positive in many ways. The key thing is that the universe responds to how you are feeling when you say the affirmation. For example, if you are using the following affirmation "the universe provides everything I need", it would be important to be feeling grateful while you are repeating this. If you truly feel resentful about not having enough money or being broke, then how you are feeling will not match your words. The universe will respond to the resentful part and the part that feels the lack with more feelings of lack. Law of attraction always responds to your vibration not your words. When you understand this, it can help you make sense of what you have attracted so far in your life.

Having said all that, these affirmations can be a powerful way to raise your vibration and begin to attract what you want in your life. Saying the affirmations aloud can be powerful as can writing them down. You will find a lot of affirmations on the internet, but it can be helpful to write your own in your own words. In this way your own affirmations hold more meaning for you. There are affirmations in the appendix of this book. You can use them immediately as they are or adapt them for your purpose.

8-Setting an intention to hear.

We will list processes in this book to help you with connecting to your guidance. We discuss intention in some detail too. If you are willing to hear from your guides, you can set an intention to connect and hear what they are saying. There are so many ways this can work and be personal to you. Some people will look for signs, for example, spotting a feather. Others may have communication with their guides through dreams. It is our promise that everyone is capable of interaction with their guides like that which Audrey enjoys. It is an inbuilt ability of each human, but the modern person's mind is very cluttered and there are some layers to work though before this is possible.

9-Being open to guidance.

This is a process because there is trust involved on both sides of the equation. You will have the opportunity as time goes by to see how our messages sit with you and whether they resonate. These will be subtle at first. You may see a feather on your path. You may be thinking of us, and a song comes on the radio. You may hear our words from the mouth of others or in books that you resonate with. Every person learns in a different way such as visually, through listening, reading or kinaesthetically. Trust that your guidance will be personal and in a form that has meaning for you.

10-Discipline to the process and acceptance of messages received

From our side it is helpful if there is a dedication to showing up to the page or to listening. It can be good to have a meditation practice that becomes part of your life. Creating space to listen and be present is important. You will develop and enhance your ability to communicate with us the more often you show up. It does not have to be for long periods. Rather it can be for 10-15 mins at a time a few times a week.

Try to be open to and accept the messages that you hear and feel. It can be important not to second guess yourself. As a rule, the communication coming from your guides and angels will be positive and be uplifting in tone and content. If what you are perceiving messages that are overly negative, then it is probably not coming from your angelic guides. Be discerning about what you hear and ask your gut if you can trust it. Be open to hearing answers and perspectives to problems that you had not expected. In the end only you can decide what sits well with you and what does not.

11-Normalisation and integration of the process and integrating it into daily life

A key part of tuning into your guidance is quieting your mind so you can hear it. There are so many thoughts that take you away from being centred. By cultivating a meditation practice it can make it easier to hear what is being communicated. It has taken time, but Audrey has very much integrated the experience of receiving our guidance into her life. It can be a bit jarring at first and she did question herself in the beginning. A key was consistency of keeping up the writing. It has come to a place where she now seeks guidance for every matter in her life of which she is unsure. She feels like she has integrated it into her life.

A time where she sought our guidance was when she was unsure about a person's motivation in a situation in her life. We revealed this to her which was very helpful. There were experiences that were very helpful for her growth that we encouraged her to attend. We aim to be uplifting and to point out her progress which she has difficulty seeing herself. These may seem like small things, but they are not. It brings a sense of peace when all your decisions are backed up by the universe. We have been delighted to see her sense of personal power increase since we have begun working with her.

CHAPTER 9

Meditations to connect you to your angels and your Higher being

The benefit of taking time in meditation is to open you up to your internal world. Inside you there is a deep well of wisdom and knowing that can be cultivated. Giving yourself time to go within allows this wisdom to rise. The effects while initially subtle, can be life changing. In your day to day, world of matter and three-dimensional living you can forget there is a way to access the whole of your being and your intuition.

In meditation the thoughts slow down, and you can begin to sense the presence that is aware of the thought, the silent watcher. Cultivating periods of silence can allow this awareness to rise. It is a profound realisation when you come to believe you are the watcher of the thoughts. This means that you are not your thoughts, and you do not have to believe everything they are telling you. You have power to decide what you give your attention to and what to ignore. From our perspective we can see that there is a collective of thoughts that are common to the whole of humanity. Thoughts of not feeling good enough are probably the most common of all. It is sad that you majestic beings with the power to create your life as you desire it, are remaining stuck because of this and other old thought patterns. We would encourage you to question your thoughts and simply ignore those that do not serve you. As you withdraw your attention from them, they are less likely to impact your life. You can also tell yourself a better story by using affirmations to positively shift your mindset.

As with everything you can test this information, we are giving you here by silently going within and stilling, the mind and body. Begin by asking your higher being what it wants you to know. Ask questions of it. Be prepared to hear the answers in a variety of ways from hearing a response, physically experiencing it, to seeing signs in your day-to-day life that help to answer the question for you. Audrey began hearing our voices through automatic writing. Have a pen and paper nearby and jot down what comes to mind. She honed her connection with us by rising early to transcribe our words for many months until she could easily connect with us at any time of day. We say this because connecting with your higher being may take time and some determination on your part. However, everyone without exception can connect to their higher being and their guides it may just take a period of discipline, an open heart and a curiosity to engage with the process.

Our intention for you when it comes to meditation is that you will be able to come more into connection with your higher being. We intend that you will have more clarity in your life and take aligned action that will result in more powerful manifestation of your desires and wishes. This was the process that you came to Earth to experience. You came to see things as they are and intend differently and manifest the improvement so that your life conditions would be exactly as you desired. Of course, this is not to say that you expected that there would never be any hard times or negative experiences. You did not fear these when you decided to reincarnate, because you knew that they would make your desire stronger and would result in learning and expansion. Next, we will explore a few common questions on meditation before proceeding with the processes.

I have tried to meditate but it hasn't worked for me. My brain seems too active. Can you help me?

We think that the processes described in this book will be helpful for you. The key is to be patient with yourself because it can take time and repetition before it becomes easier. We promise that it will. Remember to set an intention before you start that you will get what you need from it. Try to detach from any judgement of the self as it is counterproductive. Most important is patience with the self because you are learning something new, and it will take time and dedication. Even if you experience a moment of detachment that is a victory. It is also crucial that you are dedicated to set time aside at the time of day that suits you to meditate.

Different conditions such as sitting and lying can suit different people. Audrey because she has a very active mind is often very distracted during meditations. She finds guided meditations with music to be most effective for her as she detaches more easily from her thoughts. Some others may be able to achieve the same thing by sitting quietly in a room. Realising everyone is different and there is no one set prescription when it comes to meditation is key.

You speak of the benefits of meditation and describe the process. How can I ensure I am doing it right?

There is no right or wrong when it comes to meditation. If your mind gets distracted with thoughts while you are in meditation that is ok. Allow the thoughts to arise and to pass through. Judging yourself for not doing it correctly is just another stick to beat yourself with and it is defeating the purpose of the meditation in the first place.

The intention at the beginning of meditation is very important. Set yourself up in a comfortable place where you will not be disturbed. Allocate 15 minutes or so of time and relax and allow what arises to arise. Meditation can bring some emotions to the surface that may have been hidden or suppressed. It is important to allow these feelings to arise and sit with them. You will find that once you allow them to come up and give them your attention they will begin to dissipate. It is a great secret that feeling the feelings you have being trying so hard to avoid can be a simple process. By acknowledging these feelings and being compassionate with them, you allow them to fully move through and out of the body. You are also dealing with them permanently in this way as distracting and ignoring them will mean they persist. What you resist persists is a great truth.

When you first begin to feel those feelings in your body, it can be difficult as they are feelings you have ignored, numbed or avoided for many years. Feeling the feelings in the body can be very frightening. We know the intensity of the of them feel like they may drown or overcome you. Your body can cope with these feelings. This is our promise. By bringing your attention to these feelings your attention helps them shift and dissipate. Like children they are trying to get your attention, and they will not stop nudging you until you give it to them. Set the intention to expand yourself to experience the full force of the feeling, stay with the feeling even if it is uncomfortable, and allow it to pass through you. In this way you are not holding on to energy that may no longer serve you.

In paying attention to these feelings, are you not opening a can of worms? Many would be frightened of being overwhelmed by the emotions and losing control. We would say control is an illusion in any case, so it is best to dispel this myth. On the contrary, when you intend to feel your emotions no matter how uncomfortable, you will put yourself on a path to processing them and setting yourself free. The emotions persist if you do not look at them and may eventually get your attention through a crisis in health.

With the meditations below it can be a good idea to record

yourself reading them on your phone and play them back when you have time and space when you won't be disturbed.

Feeling the presence within

Go to somewhere quiet where you won't be disturbed for 10 minutes or so. Settle into a comfortable chair with your feet planted on the ground. You can also lie down if you feel more comfortable. Take three deep breaths in through your nose and out through your mouth making the exhalation longer than the inhalation. Begin to mentally think of relaxing every muscle in your body. You can start at the top of your head and work your way down to your feet. Thoughts will come to mind but allow them to pass through knowing they are just shifting energy. Try not to get attached to any single thought form. Once you feel your body has relaxed try and feel the energy in your body. A simple way to do this is to think of your hands. Can you feel the subtle energy in your hands? It can just be a tingle or a slight heaviness and that is ok. Now come into your body more fully. Feel the aliveness in them, feel sensations hot or cold, any tension are all signs of the energy in your hands. All these sensations help you feel the subtle energy of the body. Coming into the body and appreciating the energy of the body can help you to isolate this subtle energy that inhabits your body. Inhabits is a good word because your energy inhabits your body and know that this only a part of your greater energy. Feel into this energy now and allow it to expand. Sit with this energy for a few minutes and when you are ready gently open your eyes.

Communicating with your higher being

You can come to be in contact with your higher being through meditation Audrey visualises her higher being as above her head on the right-hand side. We will give you a step-by-step process below

- Sit somewhere comfortable with your back straight and your feet in contact with the floor. You can lie down with your legs outstretched. It may be better to sit up if you feel you will fall asleep when you are lying down.
- Close your eyes
- Taking 5 deep breaths make the exhalation longer than the inhalation for example breath in for 4 and out for 8 seconds
- Begin to direct you attention to different parts of your body starting with your head. Direct the muscles in each area to relax. Move down the body and finish with the feet.
- Bring you attention to the crown of your head. Imagine there is a portal from the top of your crown that is flowing light from your head outwards into the universe but also there is a thread of brilliant white light flowing back into your head.
- Allow yourself to settle for a moment. If you are sitting upright, you can visualise a thread flowing down from the soles of your feet reaching to the crystalline core of the earth. This will keep you tethered and grounded.
- Now imagine this light flowing from your crown chakra is diverting to your left or right wherever your higher being is. Go with your instinct. You may sense your higher being visually for example in the shape of a ball of light. Whatever occurs to you allow it to be. It may be more of a feeling than a vision.
- I want you now to direct the thread of light from your crown towards your higher being. You can visualise your higher being surrounded by this beautiful light. Continue this for a minute. Now as the connection has been made,

you can allow any messages to flow to you. This may take the form of images, thoughts or feelings. In the initial stages it may be a very subtle change such as a change in the temperature of your forehead, a tickle in your throat or an urge to shift position. It is most important that you don't judge anything that you receive. Remain open hearted and allow all.

- Sit with the presence of your higher being for a few minutes. Thank your higher being for all their help. Remaining in a state of gratitude is important. Disconnect your attention from your higher being and bring your attention back into the body now.

Start with little movements of your fingers and toes and move to stretching your body and moving in your chair. If you have time sit with the feeling and allow the energy to stabilise. It can be a good idea to write down any insights in your journal

Just a note here to say that you can never fully disconnect from your higher being. The connection is always there and will remain so while you are in this body. As modern life is so busy and there are so many distractions, people are often somewhat disconnected from their higher being. Communication can be enhanced by clearing the channels and focusing in as described in this exercise. Your higher being is the most amazing resource that is available to everybody. The source creator ensured that nobody is alone in this life and so everyone has guidance from their higher being but also from other sources too such as angelic guides and other guides.

Connecting with the Angels

You can try this exercise as a way of connecting with us. Sit in a comfortable chair and take a few deep breaths with longer exhalations until you feel settled. Imagine now your guardian angel standing behind you. They open their wings and enfold you in their embrace. You can feel their soft embrace. Linger in this for a few short minutes and allow yourself to feel the love your guardian angel has for you. Thank your angel.

Your guardian angel has a name. This does not matter to us as angels because it does not mean anything to us. For humans we know that a name holds significance. We are thus happy for you to name us and call upon in such a fashion. Again, this can be asked of us at periods when you are in quiet contemplation. If you do not hear the answer, ask again another time. It is not essential that you know our name to interact with us at all. Please know that we will always be holding you in our highest intention and love in any case.

Connecting with your Angels meditation 2

Go somewhere quiet where you won't be disturbed. Sit upright or lie down. Bring your attention to your breath. Allow your breathing to deepen with your exhalations longer than your inhalations. Remain for two minutes just focusing on your breathing.

- Now moving through the body from your feet up relax each part of your body focusing on each for five to ten seconds. Pay particular attention to your shoulders and your jaw. Set the intention to relax every part.
- Now visualise yourself being covered in a golden bubble of light for protection. Archangel Michael is the one who is called upon most frequently for clearing and protection. You can visualise him in whatever way he appears to you. Remember you can call on him for protection when you need to.

- See if you can get an impression of your guardian angel/s. Ask them to step forward so you can visualise them. They could appear in any form. Whether they take the shape of a human, look like an object or if you just see light, it is all ok. Allow any impression to be as it is. Sit with it for a while. Ask if there are any messages for you.
- Can you feel any subtle shift in your energy. Continue to sit in the energy for another few minutes. Thank the angels
- Thank Archangel Michael for his help and release him. Thank and release any angels or guides that appeared to you also.

*It is fine if you received no impression of your guardian angels. You are not doing anything wrong. If the intention was genuine on your part, you may find repeating the process another time is helpful. It can take time. Be open to receiving signs at a later stage. Praying to your angels can be helpful. Any practice that aims to connect with them on a daily or weekly basis will show them your dedication. In the absence of any communication from you, your guardian angel remains with you regardless.

Drawing images of your angel

If after mediation or any of the processes here, you get an image of your angel it can be helpful to draw it. Do not worry if it is only colours or for example a feather that is ok. Any impressions you get can be recorded in this way. When you are expressing yourself creatively it can be easy to release resistance and come into presence. It is important not to judge any images you sketch. They are just your impressions so allow what arises to arise without judgement.

If you have frequent impressions, it can be useful to document them in a notebook or sketch pad as it can help to have your images in one place. You may notice a progression in the imagery. Be open to what you receive in this way. If you never receive an image this is ok too. Perhaps your guides are communicating with you in different way.

Sensing the love of the angels

Your angels have so much love for you. As Audrey was finishing up this book, she was constantly reminded by us to try to convey to you the deep love that your angels have for you. It can be difficult to fully understand this from your physical standpoint. It is not a love that you need work for, as it is given unconditionally to you, just as you are. It has been a constant in your life since you came into this world, and it will move with you into non- physical when you pass over. We wish that you could feel this love not in its entirety, for it would be overwhelming, but rather in flashes or snapshots or brief moments.

We want you to come into the vicinity of this love so you can feel treasured, valued and important, for you are these things. It is a feeling more than anything solid. Some people feel it when they are in nature, and it feels as everything slows down and a peaceful feeling sets in. When awe is present so are we and we are beaming love to you in that moment when all your resistance is relinquished, and you are free. You may come across us in meditation also in those peaceful moments where it feels as if time stands still. We invite you to try the process above, of feeling an embrace from your angels. You can hone your perceptions of us as you continue to engage with us. Audrey has noticed that her visual pictures of us are becoming clearer as time goes on.

When it comes to sensing our love, can you imagine the crown of your head opening and allowing our beautiful golden light to fill your body. It can be helpful to clear your energy first by grounding down into the Earth and sending down any negative energy that no longer serves you. You can imagine us sitting opposite you are beaming you love in the form of a golden bubble. Allow this golden bubble to surround you and your aura 360 degrees above and below. Our intention is that you feel protected while basking in the glow of our love. Really it is a process of allowing our love to flow to you when you feel you are in a state of flow and non-resistance. Worry not, if you can't do this it will flow to you anyway whether you sense it or not, for it is unlimited and unconditional.

Beloved one, you shine so bright, and we see your innate power and beauty. You came forth at this time to uplift others and to help the expansion of the planet and universe and for that we are truly grateful to you.

Gratitude Practice.

We would like to emphasise that gratitude can be a wonderful practice. By finding positives in your environment, you are taking your attention off the unwanted and stopping all resistance and increasing your vibration. The vibration of gratitude is high just below love and joy.

We see gratitude as an action. It is not passive. It is a willingness to find something that pleases you. When you acknowledge the good things and people that you have in your life you are blessing all your blessings. The law of attraction will respond to this by sending you more of the same.

The highest prayer you can offer source God is thank you, for you are standing in full appreciation of your life. If you pray you can offer a prayer of gratitude during your day or when something goes well.

Having a gratitude practice does not have to be difficult or add much time to your day. It can be as simple as writing a short list of what you are grateful for in the morning. It can be great before going to sleep to jot down a few things that went well in the day. It is important to take time to acknowledge the positives but more broadly the progress that you are making overall in your life. Keeping track of little wins is important because the human brain has a propensity towards negativity. It can serve as a roadmap to show you how far you have come. Remember to thank yourself for all the effort you are putting in.

Remember the benefit of gratitude is threefold

- Takes your attention off the negative.
- Stops all resistance.
- Increases your vibration

Having a gratitude practice is a powerful way to move towards a higher frequency. Affirm gratitude when you are feeling it. Don't force it if you are feeling resentful or angry about something as your lower vibration will cancel any benefits out. It is our contention that most people can find a few things that they are grateful for. If you are stuck in negativity look for something general for example a warm breeze on your skin or how you feel comfortable in your chair where you sit. Even a small amount of time spent being grateful can cause momentum on positive thoughts and help shift your mood and vibration.

Maintaining a practice, where you notice things, you are grateful for, sets you up to be more consistently in a higher vibration. It is a good idea to do this is early in the morning when you wake up and at night before bed to set the intention for the next day. Small changes that can make a difference

- Writing down or affirming what you are grateful for as often as possible.
- Writing down what things went well at the end of every day and giving thanks for them

- Remember to acknowledge and thank yourself for all your efforts
- Expressing gratitude to the people that have supported you. Consider writing a letter of gratitude to someone who inspires or has helped you.
- Being grateful for any small seemingly insignificant thing in your life, such as a nice meal can help you shift your vibration.
- When you are grateful you are on the positive side of the coin which means you are feeling hopeful.

Remember gratitude is an active practice. Appreciation of where you are is the most effective way to welcome abundance into your life.

It may be helpful to further clarify why gratitude is important in your life with these questions.

Is being grateful in my life helpful?

Yes, this is most definitely the case. This is because the vibration level of gratitude and appreciation are high on the scale of emotions. When you are appreciating all that, you have, you are making way for more good things in your life. You are saying to the universe more of this please. Its' effects are twofold in that it raises your vibration, and it says to the universe that you are ready for more of the things you appreciate. The greatest prayer or petition you can make to source God is simply thank you. It is the most profound prayer.

There is a practice that we think can be very helpful in helping you gain momentum in the manifestation of your desire. This is to write a list of what went well in your day and what you are grateful for every day before bed. It simply sets the momentum for the next day to bring you more of the same. It can be very easy to notice the bad things that are happening in our lives or in the world in general. We have explained before that it is best to take your attention off those things that feel off or negative to you. This is often because they are of a lower vibration than you are. In giving your attention to it you are moving down the vibrational scale and away from your own alignment which is why it feels so awful. It is more effective to take your attention off it so you can maintain your alignment with your higher being.

The negative news cycle is so effective in stoking fear. It is well known that when humans are in a state of fear, they are more likely to act in certain ways. For some individuals this looks like staying stuck and not moving forwards. Being in a constant state of fear can lead to negatively categorizing others and thus lead to anger and aggression towards the other. This is responsible for many wars and acts of aggression.

Is it possible to learn from and be grateful for every experience in our lives no matter how unpleasant?

Yes, this always the case. It may be challenging for you to find anything positive about a difficult situation while going through it and this is not the point. It can be beneficial not to resist the state of reality as it is at the time. For example, if you are feeling ill, to relax into the state and rest and allow your body to heal. It is of course difficult to feel thrilled about being in bed for a few days with an acute illness when you had other plans, but it is always the best option to accept where you are at the time. Going inwards and asking the body what it needs is always important. This may seem illogical to some but when you settle into your body you should be able to feel its sensations and movement, even aches and pains. You may be hit with an overwhelming feeling of exhaustion you had not been aware of. Directing your intention inwards will give a real sense of what the body needs, and you can go from there. Honouring the body's need by rest and self-care is most wise.

We have gone slightly off topic with our example of an acute illness that blindsided you. There are many other perceived negative experiences that you could list. It is always important to ask what influence am I under? Making a judgement as to the emotion that best describes your state. If you are in a period of intense negativity, it may not be possible to find anything positive about the situation. Negative momentum may have overtaken you. It can take some momentum to get back on a positive trajectory again. You may be able to find your way into more neutral territory by appreciating something that is non-specific to what you are experience. For example, if you are extremely ill in bed you may be able to appreciate the softness and comfort of your pillow for example. If you dwell on this feeling of contentment more positive thought will be added and there will be momentum towards feeling better.

PART 2

Questions and Answers

CHAPTER 10

About angels and how they help you

Perhaps a very helpful way to answer questions about us and our existence can be through a questions and answer format. Here follows a broad range of questions. These questions are by no means exhaustive. They were those that occurred to Audrey as questions that she would like clarity on. When we answer them, we intend to put forward the truth so that our responses will be clear and easy to understand. It is our intention that this will be helpful to you in your lives. There are questions on common human problems also in the third section. We are answering those from our perspective in the non-physical plane and so we may have a different perspective to those on Earth. We wish to say that even if the questions don't apply directly to you, they still contain valuable information about the metaphysical answer to the problem.

ABOUT ANGELS.

What do you look like?

This is difficult to describe as we are ultimately energy. To those who can see us we can appear in different shapes and forms. We can appear as male or female, in different clothes or outfits. Audrey has seen guardian angels represented in different forms from females in long flowing robes, to males dressed like gladiators, to older women and as a young person rocking a mohawk hairstyle. The appearance or forms we take often hold significance to those we are with.

Does the same Angel stay as a person's guardian for all their life?

In general, this is the case. Sometimes other angels can come in to help for example when a person is going through a difficult time or needs guidance of a specific nature. For example, angels may change at times of turmoil in a person's life. If there is a special need for a skill for example the skill of writing angels may change around, or newer angels may come in. It very much depends on the person and the situation they are in.

What is it the most important thing you want us to know.?

It is that you are not alone and that we are always holding you in our highest appreciation and beaming positive energy towards you. We are with you and would love to interact with you if you are willing to engage with us.

Do angels have feelings too like humans?

Yes and no. We have mentioned before that there is a certain amount of detachment that we need to maintain. Also, we have an overview of the higher meaning of this lifetime you are going through. We would say that angels are less subject to negative emotion because of this level of detachment, and other factors that it may be difficult for us to explain to you. Of course, we do not relish when negative things happen to the humans we are with, but we do not get lost in the negative emotion attached to the situation. We are capable of states of great joy and these really are our baseline. We do celebrate your joyous occasions with you also. We have a propensity towards joy which is our default state. We are empathetic to humans and their challenges, but we cannot get lost in a pattern of negative emotions, or we would be no good to the humans that we serve.

How to angels relate to God?

Angels are a part of the oneness of all the universe. It would be wrong to see us as subordinate to the creator but rather working in unison with them. We see ourselves as extensions of their love and mercy towards humanity who without exception always have an angel nearby. We are in relation to God, as is all the universe, in that we are part of God and they are part of us. We are all one. We often pray to the source God for those we guide in life. We know the importance of prayer as we have also the perception of the other dimensions through which it flows and how it is answered. This is as best as we can explain it for now.

Is there a hierarchy of angels?

Yes, this is true. Archangels exist who oversee our functioning in general. Most humans are familiar with the archangels such as Gabriel, Michael and Raphael. There are more than those mentioned, and they have purposes that range from protection to healing and many other roles such as Archangel Melchizedek who is known as the universal overseer. The archangels came, into being to oversee all angels and to help source God advance the cause of goodness in the world.

Can little children see you more easily?

Yes, this is true. This is because small children and babies are closer to the great source and non-physical because of being recently incarnated again. They see us as images that are comfortable to them. This can persist up until the age of seven where the more logical sense comes into play. If your child mentions that they have seen something, be open with them. Allow them to discuss it without putting labels on it. They will usually have a sense of what it was themselves. There should be no fear of what they saw if it is angelic. Do not project your own fear onto them. If handled with reassurance and care on the first discussion they will be more likely to return for subsequent conversations.

Can I ask my guardian angel to contact the guardian angel of another?

Yes, this can be done. It is important to firstly develop a relationship with your own guardian angel before you can try this. You always ask that your angel ask permission of the person's higher being before there is an exchange. The intention is very important when you do this. You are never doing this to be nosy or to get information about the person. It can only be attempted if you have a genuine concern about the person. The intention is to honour the person and that any information that is revealed is for the highest good. In many cases nothing is revealed, and it is important that you respect that and do not persist in your efforts.

Where do you go when your human dies?

As we mentioned before we live in a multiverse and so can access different planes of time simultaneously. We have multiple contracts with people in the world and so when you have passed to non-physical, we have others that we are supporting. This is the best explanation we can give at this time.

Is there anything that we humans can do that can make you withdraw from us?

No, as we have said we don't see you in those terms. We only hold you in our attention as the highest version of yourself. Also, as we mentioned before, we do not blame or criticise. you as this is not possible because we are too high a vibration to engage in criticism or judgement.

Can you interact with our deceased loved ones?

Yes, because of the nature of the universe we all inhabit, universal laws do permit this. We see ourselves as separate entities to those who have transitioned to the non-physical plane. This is again due to frequency but to other factors too. In simple terms, we can give messages to your deceased loved ones and transmit their messages too. It is not everyone who can receive these messages, for not everyone is at a frequency to hear us, but if you pray to us and request it, we can send your messages on.

How can I know the name of my guardian angel?

It can be a good idea to ask when your mind is quiet such as in meditation or just afterwards. Ask and be willing to sit and listen. It may take a little time to be revealed to you. Listen with an open heart and trust what you hear.

Have you been in physical form before?

Most of us have not walked the Earth in physical form before. In some cases, some people have guides that having come to the end of their time of earth do become guardian angels. We understand that this needs to be allowed by the Archangels and does not occur often. The being who has returned to non-physical has to be of a high vibration and have much wisdom also to qualify. They cannot guide anyone who was alive when they were on Earth. Sometimes they guide new babies that are born into a family that they were a part of. These guides almost always have a connection with the soul they will be guiding whether from a past life or family tree.

How do you differ to other non-physical entities?

We are indeed different to others such as ancestors, Archangels and ascended masters. We are of a pure high vibrational energy that resembles the archangels and source God. It is difficult to explain as we are more of an energetic make up than anything physical that you can relate too. We are very close to the energy of source God and the Archangels.

I have not ever been aware of my angel does that mean I don't have one?

This is not the case for your angel exists whether you believe them to or not. Your impressions and beliefs are immaterial when it comes to your guardian angel. You can be sure also that your angel is influencing you to a certain degree, through what you are being drawn to at the time. We describe processes for getting in touch with your guardian which you may like to try if you would like to connect with them.

Does it matter to my angel whether I believe in them or not?

Ultimately no it does not matter to the angels whether you believe or not. They do not operate from an ego level and so are not insulted or disappointed by any of your actions. We would love you to connect more with us and be comforted by our messages which this book is all about.

I am not religious, should I still believe in angels?

We do not wish to tell you what you should believe in. We can only tell you that we exist and that you are loved and guided. We have described processes to connect with us. It can be a as simple as keeping an open mind or perhaps asking your angel to send you a sign. Keep an open mind and sees what occurs. Your heart will guide you the most in this matter.

Do angels like music?

This is a wholehearted yes especially anything uplifting and invigorating. We often send messages from ourselves and sometimes deceased loved one through songs that the person is exposed to. This may seem far-fetched, but we reassure you that this is true.

Should we pray to the angels?

You can of course pray to the angels and archangels for your intentions, and we will intercede with the source for you. It is especially good to pray to be able to receive guidance from your angels. We are always wanting to help you in whatever way that we can and want to know that we are there.

You may be answered in the form of signs or getting impulses to go to a certain place or to meet with a certain person. It may not always seem logical to you but know that we are there and working to help you in the background. As we always see you as your true whole being we are always appreciating you and beaming wellbeing to you. What we do is more active than a passive process.

CHAPTER 11

Angelic perceptions of humans

Am I known to Source/God and the Angels?

Yes, of course you are. You are a part of the whole of creation and God's creation would not be whole without you. Your being and welfare are important to us, and we know you personally, though you may not know us. Audrey was surprised when she started to write down our guidance at how personal it was. After a while she could ask for advice on any topic and she would have it instantly. We are interested in helping you at this level if you so wish. The guidance that Audrey can access is granted to all of you without exception. It starts with being open to receiving it. Taking small steady steps towards that goal then by meditating and other processes mentioned in this book. We want you to know that we are always with you whether perceived by you are not. We are always seeing the whole of your being in all its glory and are beaming wellbeing towards you.

Are prayers heard?

Yes, without doubt they are heard and what is more they are answered immediately. It may be in the form of energy that is later to be manifested. Prayers for other people take on the energy that is often sent to them. They have a very real energetic effect. It cannot be seen by your eye, but we can perceive this phenomenon. If you pray for a person who is sick and they subsequently go on to die, then you may assume that your prayer has not been heard. This would be incorrect. As mentioned before everyone has a life path with certain things set in stone. The time of death is one of these. Your prayer has positively affected them and may affect the nature of their passing or have granted them grace to face death with courage. Prayers are powerful and they are heard and responded to just not in a linear fashion that makes sense to you.

When prayer is answered in energetic form it can be difficult for you to see the effects of it, and you may remain frustrated. We say just pray with an open heart and a sincere wish for whatever you desire and then let go. Frustration is resistance and it will slow down any manifestation.

The greatest prayer that you can make is simply thank you. By appreciating the goodness in your life and truly being grateful this allows more goodness in. You do not need to praise the creator for they have no need of flattery because they have no ego. Thank you however communicates an acceptance of what is and a willingness to find the positives in any situation. The feeling of intense gratitude can be so serene and being in oneness with all that is that is a beautiful state to aspire to.

There is no judgement on the nature of your prayer nor a hierarchy of prayer. It is perfectly appropriate for you to pray for yourself as you would others. Keeping then communication open between you and source God is a wonderful thing to do. In conclusion, all prayers are heard and answered though not always in the way that your mind may expect.

If angels really exist and are protecting us why are some people's lives so miserable?

This is an excellent question. When you as a spiritual energy decide to reincarnate into a body for a new life the broad arc of the life you will lead is revealed to you, for example your family and your country of origin and the major events of this lifetime. You agree to a contract to reincarnate into that body in that time and space dimension with the intention of learning and expansion of yourself and the whole of creation. Believe it or not this is seen as a very exciting prospect by your higher being, as you relish the opportunity to be enmeshed in the newness of life with the potential to learn and expand. Even though the key events of the life ahead are revealed there is always personal choice in how a person chooses to react to events, as they have of course choice to shape their life as they would wish. This is not a contradiction even though it may sound like one.

Even though to the outward eye some lives may seem particularly unfortunate or full of suffering the person on the outside cannot know the inner experience of the individual. There can be much joy in the lives of people whom the outside world would view as suffering or miserable. You cannot know the lessons that the person came to learn in that life nor of the contract they agreed to on reincarnating. We say to take your eye off their suffering and see them as the whole person they are. See them in their greatness as everyone has greatness on the inside. Of course, to pray for such a person is helpful but do not do so out of pity but more with the intention to uplift them.

It is not the path of the angel to change predestined states or events rather to support and help the person in whatever capacity they can. Audrey, if she has a decision to make, asks for guidance from her group. It has been transformative for her as she now has clarity that she never knew before. As a result, she is taking action that is aligned with her higher being and her angels. A few times recently when she did not take time to write before a decision, she was pleasantly surprised that they affirmed her choice while saying that the habit of automatic writing had meant that almost all her actions were aligned with her higher goals. Audrey knows this is a wonderful place to be because to her clarity is as valuable as gold. The benefit in never having to second guess herself alone has been immense.

It is our promise that every human on this planet is not alone and has a guardian angel. We ask that you use this resource by being in contact with your angel and being open to hearing their guidance.

Why do you want to help humans?

For some of us we were human ourselves and we know that it can be lonely at times. Most of us non-physical guides have not been physical before. Like you we were created by source God to serve and protect you as a mechanism of support. This system was put into place because of the great love the creator has for you. It is difficult to describe all the purposes we serve because time is non-linear where we are, so the role can be multi-faceted. We do enjoy our jobs, and we have subtle ways of guiding those who we are not in direct communication with. We come from a place of love and have great love for you.

Can you ever intercede with a human to change their path?

We cannot do so because humans have free will. It is not our role to participate in such work. Though we have great love for you we maintain detachment from your life situation and understand that events will play out as they will. We are also able to see the bigger picture, for example in the case of great suffering, we see the purpose of this, such as, fulfilling karmic debts or for growth of the soul. It is not for us to judge. We are standing beside you always beaming wellbeing to you.

If you can see the bigger picture, you may see the ways we sabotage ourselves. Does what we do or don't do frustrate you?

It is true that many of your actions do work against what you ultimately want. We have no feelings either way about this. As mentioned before, we do not get caught up in emotions as we are detached from them. We will often do our best to send you signs if we feel we can help you, but really there is no worry or anguish on our part. We know you have multiple lifetimes to complete what you need to do. We have mentioned that time is not linear like you perceive it to be. For us, you can never get it wrong, and you can never get it all done in this lifetime This is because experiences are learning devices. Therefore, we ask you to relax. Allow yourself to reach the state of appreciation for your life and what all that you do. We are constantly in this state. From this state of appreciation, you can create more easily what you would like.

How can I begin to have an interaction with my guardian angel?

In essence this is what this entire book is about. The most important factor is intending it to be so. This is discussed at length in the body of the book. Clearing of mental clutter is important and the processes are described within. Developing and maintaining a meditation practice is also extremely important in helping to quiet the mind, so that guidance can be heard, felt and experienced. Being consistent in your processes is extremely important as this shows your guides that you are serious in your intention and that you will follow through. Angels speak to you in many ways such as leaving feathers, birds and messages in songs on the radio The methods become less subtle as you begin to engage directly with us. We wish to say that everyone is capable of this interaction and indeed we are joyful at the prospect of interacting with you in any way that you choose. We will never overwhelm or frighten you and in all cases this information will come to you in a way that is comfortable and meaningful to you.

Why do angels hold humans in such high esteem when the evidence in the world is that humankind can be unspeakably cruel to our fellow man and indeed the planet too.

We hold you in high esteem because we can see the whole of you including the part that remains non-physical. We know that your essence is pure love. The negative events that are playing out on earth stem from wrong perception that the self is separate and alone. This allows humans to perceive the others as separate and so to condemn them. It is a great truth of our universe that all is one. That is everything and everyone, God included, are all part of a whole. When action is taken from this place of wholeness, you could never hurt another as to do so, would mean hurting yourself.

We also admire that you came into the physical world in this time space continuum. You undertook this with the intention of self-expansion, and you are contributing to the expansion of the whole and we are grateful to you for this.

I feel so lonely; can you help with this?

We wish to tell you that you are never alone for not only do you have guides in the non-physical plane that are with you always. The feeling of loneliness occurs when you are feeling the distance between yourself and your higher being which is the whole of you or total you. Your higher being is the sum of all you have lived in all your past lives. It is the totality of all your wisdom a result of your lived experiences on Earth yet also your knowledge of the nature of the universe.

We explored connecting with your higher being in a meditation earlier. Give yourself time to become used to meditation. At times, when you are feeling like time stands still or you are overcome with joy or bliss you and your higher being are fully in unison. Having a meditation practice can be immensely helpful when it comes to cultivating this connection. This connection has the potential to help you in profound ways, and it can be a gamechanger when you are operating in unison with your higher being. This is a natural state and not something that needs to be forced. It is about creating the space and allowing the communication to begin. It will take time and patience, but you can feel your way towards it. When you reach that state even briefly you may feel immense relief and joy.

Most humans are not aware of their higher being and so cannot operate from a position of unity. Also, we would say it is not possible for most to maintain this state ongoing indefinitely. Of course, there will be fluctuation because your world contains so many distractions and many of you are in states of doing. It is easier to access the state of being united with your higher being when you are at a higher frequency or vibration or feeling good. Affirmations can help you move into a place of feeling better. Pick the best feeling thought that you can. It is all momentum and the longer you can stay with that thought the most likely that the next thought will also be a positive one. This can take practice, but it is very effective.

Finally, the purpose of this book is for you to establish a connection with your angel guides through the processes we have described. If you can begin with this. The guidance and clarity that can result once there is effective communication is massive. It is also a huge relief to know that you are guided in the world. The truth is there are many things you can do to feel less lonely. It starts with a better feeling thought and bringing yourself to a place where you can begin to move towards your guidance. We promise that we never leave you and we are always beaming wellbeing towards you. you simply must get yourself in a slightly better feeling place and begin to allow the process of opening to us. It is comforting to know that everything is working out for you in this moment. The sum of your experience in this life and past lives have led you to this place in this time and space continuum which is perfect and exactly as it should be. All is going well for you.

I don't always understand your language and words. What can I do?

The words used in this book have been chosen deliberately to best explain to you on a mental and subconscious level the greater concepts we are describing. We have tried to keep them as simple as possible and to repeat ourselves so we can clarify concepts. It does not matter if you do not always understand our words, for we are teaching on a vibrational level too which is at the level of the metaphysical. You may not understand on a mental level, but it is our intention that other parts of you will respond and integrate our teachings on all levels of your very complex being.

Do angels assist the dying?

Yes, this is a part of the role of angels to help with the transitions of humans to the next world. Those open to having us with them will see us then. There are cases where resistance from humans means that it is not possible for angels to become involved. This is usually to do with the person feeling stuck and them not being ready to move on to the next life and so the resistance is greater than the will of the helper angel. The angels wish for you to know that this an important part of our role and to please call upon us in the hour of your passing or beforehand. We want you to know we are available to help you with this, and we want you to call us to your side (we will be there anyway) in your last days. Of course, many people will not have notice before they pass away, for example in the case of accidents. We can help you offload complex emotions and surrender to the process. We will be there in any event. There is nothing you need do.

Is there something you would like us to know about looking after our bodies?

You broadly know how to take care of your bodies daily. There is an abundance of knowledge in the public consciousness about what habits and practices are good and nourishing for the body. There is also much information available on practices that do not serve your body and your general health. We therefore do not need to be prescriptive in our answer. If you persist with habits that may not be healthy for your body, it can be interesting to ask yourself why? You do not need to change anything just become aware of your motivation to act in these ways. Reflect on this and be aware. Your body holds much wisdom if you are prepared to go within and listen.

Can angels help me to heal my body?

Yes and no. This is more of an indirect way. We do not perform the miracle of healing in our direct capacity. The body has many mechanisms to heal itself and we would like to ask you to bring your focus back to the body and send it love and blessings. Going within in meditation can open you up to the internal wisdom of the body also. Your higher being always has insights on how to heal yourself and will lead you to the right people to help you do this. There is an old saying "if you don't go within, you go without". We would like to say that going within in, by meditating can help you access the wisdom of your higher being and your soul. The body also has innate wisdom that you can become conscious of if you tune in to it. You often give away your power by deferring to others who look only at the physical body when trying to heal you. The body contains the physical, emotional, mental and spiritual components and unless they are all addressed there can be no lasting healing.

Can angels tell the future?

Yes, we can see a broad overview of what is ahead for you and the world in general. We do not always subscribe to the view that knowing these things benefit you. Of course, there are those among you who can know these things naturally through your own gifts. When we speak with Audrey, we can advise her on a general course of action with the likely outcome. It, of course, does help to know that she is acting in alignment with us and her higher being. In many instances people seek help from psychics as they may not be in tune with their own internal wisdom. There is much wisdom your higher being can share with you. It can help to develop a meditation practice to become more open to this guidance.

One thing that we really want to stress is that you come into this world with an amazing guidance system, your gut reaction. This is present in everyone from birth. Living in a family where parents may be guiding you in addition to teachers and other mentors, some people begin to override their own innate guidance system. A classic example is in dealing with relationships. A person may get a gut feeling about another person but may override this in the interests of being polite or appearing likeable. They may go on to put themselves in a vulnerable position with someone they did not get a good feeling about in the first place. We would recommend you honour your gut instinct as it is always right. It is of benefit to teach the younger generation also that it is important to listen to this instinct and not override it. We are sure that many among you, can name times when they discounted their initial instinct in relation to a person, company, workplace or situation and came to regret it later. We say foster this gut instinct or guidance system, listen to it and act accordingly. It is a wonderful tool to help you navigate this world.

Our final word on this topic is that most humans do not truly understand the power that they possess. We wish to say that you are a powerful co-creator with the universe. You can be, do or have anything that you desire. It can be hard to hear this if your life is not going the way that you hoped. However, it is true, and if you look at the process of manifestation already discussed, anything can be possible for you. Impossible- the word itself says I'm Possible. This is a big shift in mindset to what is taught in your society and school, but it is not false. It will take a certain amount of focus on the things that you want and dwelling on the feeling that what you desire is already here. Changing your expectations is another component but that is really it. You employ this process for many things of lesser importance to you every week and it works perfectly well but with the bigger things there are bigger mental blocks, and this can mean they will take longer to come. If we could sum it up in one sentence, we would say spend time thinking about what you want and how it will feel when it does come to you.

Can angels save humanity from its fate?

We are always working to help humanity in the best way that we can. We don't think of any fate as being set in concrete as everything is in flux. We are influencing you as and we are always shining a beam of wellbeing in you and seeing you as your highest and most powerful self. We believe this has a positive influence on you. We don't see humanity as needing to be saved. From our vantage point we can see all the wellbeing that is at play in your universe. We see the expansion of your planet and the evolution of consciousness that is now taking place. We are optimistic because we can appreciate the true beauty of the world and universe that you live in.

Many religions would see me as a sinner. Is this how you look upon us in general?

This is not the case. There is no such judgement. We would say that many of your books of worship the words have been twisted against Source God and against yourselves. It is a truly loving God that sent us to be with you. They could not countenance you being on your own in the world, even for a minute. Does this sound like a judgemental, condemning God to you? For this is not God. Source God sees you as a magnificent being who has the freedom to create what you want to be, do or have. You have all the tools to do this. You are loved and guided every moment on this earth, a love that you often resist because you do not feel worthy. You were given an inbuilt guidance system to help you with what you prefer. This works also to tell you what is right or wrong.

Not that this is a big consideration for source God, because there is no hell after this life, and you will not be punished no matter what you perceive your crimes to be. Your guidance system alerts you when something is off. We would say to you that this guidance is letting you know the distance between you and your higher being and sometimes also the great source. When you feel awful about something it is often because you have cut yourself off from your higher being. For example, when you are hating on yourself there is a discrepancy in how you feel about yourself and how they feel about you.

We have told you that your higher being is always sending you a stream of positive energy and only sees you as whole and complete. When you feel down on yourself there is a split in the energy between you and your higher being. It does not matter what you feel your higher being will continue to beam that positive energy towards you in a constant stream. You can wallow in your bad feeling but your higher being well never change the way that they feel about you. Conversely the times you are feeling excited and joyful and unlimited, you are in sync with your higher being and so the energy flows beautifully between you. When you are in this state you are united with your higher being, your whole self and source God. There is no resistance. That is why it feels so good. Also, when you are in this state you have the power of the whole of your being to create and that is why it is a powerful time to set intentions and bring focus to what you want to occur.

Considering this, we would say to you to care about how you feel. Look for the best feeling thought and then and build the momentum of the good feeling. If you are feeling down or low, it is not the time to create. Rather do what you can to feel the best you can. If this is not possible then the momentum will pass when you take a nap or after a sleep.

If angels can't interfere with our life path or have any impact on our decisions what good are they to us ultimately?

This is a very good question. Of course, we do try and influence you in subtle and not so subtle ways for those of you who are in contact with us directly. We think of ourselves as gently guiding you. It is true that knowledge can be found within yourself. That is to say that there is true wisdom to be gained by going within. We are the whisperers along your path. We are gently leaving a trail to follow. There is always free will for humans so you may often have to make decisions in which there are better choices than others. We try to gently lead you to the better choice. There is no consequence of not following our guidance as there is no punishment apart from that which you might experience on the physical plane. We, like your higher being, are always beaming positivity towards you and seeing you as your most majestic self. If a lesser path is taken, we will stay focused on the whole of who you are and continue to hold you in our highest regards.

We also are with you when you are going through tough times in your life. In our own way we pray for you and hold you in our positive gaze. We have had to, for a few humans to intercede with source God on their behalf. We are with you at the hour of your death also, which is a time that it is necessary to have a guide to the non-physical plane. Guiding your soul, at that time, is our final task we perform with you. It can take reassurance because many of the newly deceased are uneasy and worried and they need help and guidance. Once you are returned safely to your proper place in the universe our job is done.

We want to have a relationship with you, and we urge you to pray to us or ask us for help in whatever way seems most natural to you. We promise that you will be heard, and we will do our best to intervene, if this is possible. Even if you never speak to us, nor wish to, we are constantly working behind the scenes to help and support you. To those who don't believe us, your resistance will block any engagement with us and will repel our presence but never send us away. If you open your heart or begin to believe in the possibility of our presence, we promise that you will begin to see signs of us and you will know that we are with you, and that we love you.

Are you bored with staying with me throughout my life because sometimes my life feels boring?

It is difficult to explain this to you in this place where time seems very linear. In fact, we are multi-dimensional beings, and we can be across several other dimensions at the same time. Of course, if we just had to stay with you that would be ok with us too. Remember we love you and always intend the best for you. Also, we are in a place of detachment about your life situation, so we do not experience the intense emotions that you experience. We feel closeness to you and love for you and so we like to spend time in your company. It is not a chore.

CHAPTER 12

The Universe from our viewpoint

Is God male or female?

Source God is an energy, that would not conform to the shape of your bodies, in the physical world and so the most accurate answer is neither. However, source God is part of you as you are a part of the whole of which they exist and created. Therefore, at any time they are male and female and animal or creature. Every part of this world is a part of God and God is a part of it all. This may be difficult to understand but it is the closest to the truth we can put into words.

How did this planet come into existence?

It was a combination of your two theories of creation. Yes, there was a big bang that brought the universe into existence but there was a greater consciousness that decided to begin that process in the first place. Your scientists are very aware of the mechanism of how this planet came into existence, but they still know very little about the nature of the universe.

Is believing in God and Angels and benevolent creator or source at odd with Evolution?

It is amusing to the source creator that there are camps that believe either in evolution or creation theories. Of course, it took both creationism and evolution to have created the world we see before us today. This is because in the beginning there was only the source, and all creation flowed from their will that it be so. Consequently, evolution has created and the shaped the world we now see before us.

Then the answer to this question is that a belief in a creator of the universe is not at odds with the theory of evolution.

What is the nature of the universe?

The universe is always expanding. Your experience and the experience of all who are living currently are adding to the expansion of the universe. We want you to know that simply by living life, you are adding to the whole. This is why we hold you in such high esteem. We know that by agreeing to be on Earth, currently, you are adding to the expansion of the universe. We are so grateful for you all that you do.

When you really allow this to sink in you will realize that no mistakes are possible. There is no such thing as perfection. There must be opposites to create the contrast which leads to expansion. If you never experienced sadness, how could you possibly appreciate joy. Living through contrast or negativity can mean that you appreciate the joyful times even more. There is not one thing but two polarities to every emotion. Ask yourself what side are you on?

There are many truths to the universe that you may not be able understand when you are in this body but that will be perfectly clear to you once you make your transition to non-physical. This is when you will be whole again, united with the whole of your being and possessing all the knowledge you have gained from your many lifetimes, and your experience of existing on the non-physical plane. At that time, it will be more of a question of remembering. It is already known by your higher being. You are a being that has many lives and may continue to reincarnate once this life is over. These lives take place simultaneously as there is a multiverse of different realities.

Time as you know it here on earth does not really exist. The nearest you can come to the feeling of timelessness in this life is meditating. During meditation, when time is suspended and you feel at one with all that is, is the strongest representation of what being nonphysical is. If borne in mind this can be a powerful motivation to meditate.

Your higher being holds all these truths and has records of all the lives you have lived since the beginning of your journey. Some refer to these as the akashic record, which hold the details of all your previous lifetimes. This is why we recommend you meditate with your higher being as so much knowledge and wisdom is stored in this record.

How many dimensions there are?

Of course, it is difficult to understand the makeup of the universe while you are in physical form in a physical body. There are an infinite number of dimensions, more than your brain can comprehend. There is no exact number we can share here.

Can people communicate with us from the other realms when they have died?

Yes of course. They can find many ways to communicate with you which are significant to you and so if you can be open to this happening you can connect. While they have passed to non-physical, they still maintain a very strong interest in what you are doing. Not only that, but they are also beaming so much love to you. They are more powerful in the afterlife and so they really are focusing their love on you and wanting the best for you. From their place in non-physical they are pure love, and they are directing the flow of love to you. You can continue to interact with your loved one knowing that they hear you and that they want to interact with you.

You speak about vibration. What is this and how does it apply to me?

Everything in the universe has an energy both living and not living. Vibration as we speak of it relates to your predominant energy at a space in time. All emotions have vibrations. The more positive the emotion the higher the vibration. Shame and depression have the lowest vibration while love and joy have the highest. We know your emotional state is constantly fluctuating. This the normal state of things. We want you to know that you can move to a higher vibration by setting your intentions for each part of the day. Meditation in the morning can also be hugely helpful in setting your vibrational state for the day. This is because momentum can have a compounding effect on how your day turns out. Meditating and setting positive intentions for the day can start you on a higher vibration and the momentum of this will carry into your day. Conversely, it is possible to be assailed with negative thoughts early in the morning leading to emotions of disheartenment and depression. The first half hour when you wake up is therefore hugely important to set the tone for the day. This is because the law of attraction is predominant. This means you attract states of emotion, events and people that are in sync or a similar vibration to whatever vibration you are.

The vibration that you are projecting out into the world is like a radio signal from a transmitter. It lets the universe know exactly where you are at in that moment in time. As the universe responds to that signal it sends you people and events that align with that signal because the law of attraction must pair like with like. Changing the signal you transmit changes the people and circumstances that you attract to yourself. It is most difficult when you are transmitting a mostly negative signal to change the circumstances of your life. Negativity gains momentum and snowballs and in this place, it is impossible to get to a higher vibration without changing that momentum. This can take time because of the momentum of the prior negativity. Things that can break the momentum are meditating but that may not be possible if the mindset is extremely negative. The other thing is taking a nap or a night's sleep and meditating and intending first thing in the morning.

What is my dominant vibration?

It is always important to ask yourself what your dominant vibration is as this is the signal you put out into the world. Ask this numerous times in the day. This information is not given to you so you can judge yourself and blame yourself for perhaps not being in a place of positivity. It is important to say that emotional states are constantly fluctuating, and it is not possible for most to constantly remain in a place of positivity, in fact surrendering or letting go judgement of yourself is so important. If you are not vibrationally where you want to be that is ok. You can work towards that goal gradually. There will be progress and regressions too because that is the nature of the human experience. Everyone will experience negative events, situations and people from time to time. It is advantageous to see these events and issues as an incentive to help you create what you desire. By intending in opposition to what you already manifested you can start to shift the momentum.

It is important to be easy with yourself in relation to where you are at. Blame and frustration will send you further down the emotional scale. Many thought patterns have momentum because you have been thinking them so long and this can take time to reverse. If you can appreciate all your experiences in life, it can be helpful. Even your negative emotions and experiences can help increase your desire which is an important component in the process of co creation with the universe to fulfil your desires.

It is ok to acknowledge that you are not where you want to be on any topic but then take your attention off it because it can play into negative momentum otherwise. There are so many things that are going well for you every day, but it can be a predisposition to focus on the things that are not. It can be helpful to write down those things that you appreciate and are grateful for regularly. The feeling of appreciation is a on a high vibration so by feeling this you are moving up the emotional scale. It is important to say you cannot feel opposing emotions at the same time. For example, you cannot feel appreciation and be in a state of depression. We also like the idea of a gratitude journal that highlights your appreciation for the positives in your life.

If you can learn to be aware of your emotional state and predominant emotion, you can work towards moving up the emotional scale. By becoming more aware of this, you will notice the vibration of others around you. You will notice, those who are uplifters, and those who are not. You then have the power to choose whom you spend time with, the places you go and the situations you put yourself in. This can transform not just your energy level but how your life unfolds.

I am not where I want to be now in my vibration, how can I change?

A key factor in this dilemma is to understand how much momentum you have going on the feeling that you now are feeling. If it is early in the day and you have just woken up, it will likely be easier to tackle than if you have had the full day of allowing the negative feelings to snowball. When there is a momentum going on a topic it can be difficult to reverse everything in the opposite direction. Sometimes this can't be done in a day. Sleeping and naps provide a natural break in momentum. If you can be easy with yourself and allow things to be as they are this can be helpful. Resistance against the thoughts and feelings will only prolong the episode. Meditation is a natural breaker of momentum too, so we suggest this as a daily practice for you. Reassure yourself that nothing is going wrong and it won't last forever and be kind to yourself.

Does the vibration of other people, places and situations affect me? I refer to those that may be of a lower vibration.

The truth is that they need not affect you if you are in alignment with your higher being and/or source God. It is true, even if it is difficult to believe, that as you go through life, you need not be affected by another in any way. Indeed, if you can take your attention off anything that is upsetting to you, this in time helps to reduce its momentum. Many of the negative feelings that you have are because there is a disconnect between how you feel and how your higher being feels about an issue. The negative feeling comes because you are disconnected from the whole of your being. For example, you may feel that you detest an individual. This feels uncomfortable to you because it is not in alignment with what your higher being or indeed God feels about this person. They do not share this view because they come from a place of love. It feels bad to you because you are disconnected from the entirety of your being and not because you feel unloving thoughts towards that person.

Of course, there are times when others can uplift your vibration or lower it. On many occasions this is not deliberate on the part of the other. We urge you to use the processes mentioned above to clear and ground your energy as a way of buffering against this. You can ask your guardian angel to put to you in a bubble of protection once the clearing has been done.

Many of you can feel the vibration of the place that you are entering almost instantaneously. You often get a bad or good vibe from a place by using your instinct. In almost all cases your impressions are correct. You can choose to react to this information as you wish. We suggest spending more time in uplifting places can be beneficial.

When it comes to situations in your life, you always get an impression of them, for example you may feel a knot in your tummy. You may be able to sense the energy in a room. As always, we ask you to act in accordance with your guidance in relation to this information. Tune into it and see how it makes you feel. Once you have this information you can make a decision that is in alignment with your higher being

Can we ever know about our past lives while in this body?

With the intention of giving you a new fresh life, each time you reincarnate a veil is drawn across your ability to perceive past lives. We have explained that when you incarnate the greater part of you remains in non-physical, your higher being. This part of you has full knowledge of the whole of your life experiences. Your higher being retains access to the records of your soul journey. When incarnating to the physical plane your vibration can reduce because of becoming denser in form.

It is very much a deliberate design to allow life to unfold as you desire it to without the weight of past lives interfering. Coming into the physical plane with this knowledge would be extremely overwhelming and difficult. It would not be for your highest good in this life. It would stifle your creativity and your power to attract in your current life.

We would also say the time you have come back to Earth is significant. Not only are you growing and expanding as an individual you come at a time of huge growth and expansion for all humanity. Under these conditions expansion is significantly speeded up. What you can achieve vibrationally can be unlimited. Achieving vibrationally is always the precursor to manifesting physically. This is why you need to be concerned with you vibration and how you feel.

While you may not always be able to directly access the full history of your past lives while on the physical plane there is a mechanism whereby you can have the benefit of this knowledge. Your higher being knows all that you are and the history of your soul and is a product of the expansion and wisdom of all your lifetimes. You can cultivate a relationship with your higher being through meditation. When you do this or develop a relationship with us, as Audrey has, it can mean you are no longer in the dark searching for meaning. You are guided and have backup and answers for all your questions. More than that, it means that you are taking aligned action so your chances of success are much higher.

If you were to look back over your past lifetimes, you would see a mixed bag in terms of expansion and wisdom gained. As mentioned, the times during which you lived in can greatly influence the outcome too. All times, however, do allow the possibility to create what you want, that is, to help you manifest. All lifetimes no matter how short add to the expansion and wisdom of the soul, not to mention the expansion of the collective. This is why we see you as the magnificent beings. We admire you for living in the space time continuum and adding to the whole through your expansion. For this reason, you can never get it wrong because your experience leads to your desires which leads to your manifestation which adds to the expansion of the whole. Your difficult times are especially productive in increasing your desire for the opposite of your situation at the time. For this reason, we would say even the hardest times are to be appreciated for their power to create what you desire. When you get to a place you appreciate all experience whether negative or positive that is enlightenment.

What happens during a near death experience?

In a near death experience the soul has left the body and crossed over into another dimension but remains tethered to the body with a cord. The soul experiences a feeling of unconditional love as it is adjacent to but not fully integrated with the higher being. A feeling of lightness too is experienced because of the separation from the heavier mass that is the body. It is routine to see a loved one or a bright light. This is an experience of what the afterlife is like but almost a watered-down version. Often the peace that the soul feels is overwhelming. Some who have returned to Earth have said that at the time they would have liked to remain there and not return. Those who have returned are told they must do so and so they re-enter their bodies.

All those who have experienced a near death event change their outlook on life. Most become less fearful of death, and they begin life again with a renewed sense of purpose. We want to say that what people report frequently in these events is very much real and cannot be explained by a lack of oxygen to the brain or any other such phenomenon. They have a real taste of the dimension they will go to after they die and their experiences on this plane are meaningful. There can be many lessons learned from such experiences.

Many of those that have had these experiences go on to talk about them or write books on the subject. Their lives are never the same again because they do not fear death. They know that sharing their experience is helpful for all humanity and proof of a loving universe.

What would happen to humanity if the world was to end?

Death is not the opposite of birth; the energy that is you continues to exist on a different plane when your life on Earth ends. In a mass extinction event, the energy of the people would not be obliterated, it would simply go on to exist on another plane. We cannot explain to you what such a surge of energy would look like. From our point of view, it would be truly magnificent. We do not mean to sound as if we are glamorising such an event because we know that it is many of your worst fear however, we want you to know that it would only lead to a new and phenomenal creation. We would say that is not a fore telling of doom because that chapter of the Earth's history is very much unwritten.

You mention that we are all part of the whole of creation. If we are all connected, does this mean that what is happening in other parts of the world could affect us directly?

The simple and accurate answer is yes. We need to explain how this inter connectivity works so you can fully appreciate mechanism that is at play here. You are all part of an interconnected grid or forcefield of energy, it has been described at various times as a mesh, grid or wave of energy. These are all good descriptions but cannot possibly describe what is impossible to fully perceive at the level of this earth plane where you reside. This is something that you know as your soul has experienced the fullness of this mechanism when you were in non-physical. Moreover, you had the potential to truly understand and appreciate its magnificence when you were there. The slowing down of vibration to come into the world of matter, leaves you less able to appreciate it in its totality nonetheless it exists and predominates.

There are many who speak of this phenomenon as the collective unconscious. This is described as the whole of the mental patterns of the entire of humanity at this moment on Earth. Most humans can understand this concept well. It however is not the whole truth when it comes to the Wave* as we will call it for the purpose of discussion. The wave does not just contain the current collective consciousness of humanity but everything that has been added since the planet began and in fact before then in the pre creating phase. This encompasses all events, individual lifetimes, reincarnations, experiences and happenings. It is everything that is and was and will be on all planes of existing past present and future and beyond time and space. Time is a concept that does not exist when applied to the multiverse and all the ongoing planes of reality perceived and unperceived. It cannot be fully described in words. Your soul knows this place for it is where you return to when you die.

All events and experiences ongoing in your world at present are happening within the wave, this is why a war that is happening hundreds of miles away can affect you. Their sorrow is your sorrow because it is the collective sorrow. A universal law is all is one. Everything is interconnected. It may seem unbelievable to you that you could be affected in this way, but it is law, it just is. For example, does war in the middle east explain why millions of Americans are afflicted with sadness and taking anti-depressants? To the human eye there appears no correlation but at a metaphysical level we see the collective well of grief and sorrow send ripples throughout the collective wave throughout the world. It must manifest somehow.

Indigenous tribes have always known of this phenomenon. They live their lives only taking what they needed from the Earth and honouring the land. They entered war with extreme sadness with the wish only to protect their own way of life which they were largely unsuccessful at doing. They knew the repercussions for their tribe in terms of the long-term suffering after conflict and the potential to affect generations as yet unborn which you now describe as epigenetics.

There are those who would prefer to continue to live in a bubble pretending that their actions do not affect others in any way and claim that they are uninfluenced by their environment. We would say that is fine, but it is a law that ALL IS ONE and it exists whether you believe it does or not. It exists and operates independently of the bubble you create for yourself. We say, do not believe yourself to be uninfluenced by it because this is not possible, it is law.

You are interconnected with all life forms on your planet. When you recognise this, it may or may not lead to a change in behaviour. Buddhism has the concept of karma that is what you put out into the world will come back to you at some point. When you act against the whole or another you act against yourself, suffering ensues. It speaks to this law but does not of course fully describe the consequences on the physical, non-physical and metaphysical planes.

The flip side of the All is One law is that there is the potential for massively increased joy and love in your life when you realise the potential of this law. By avoiding actions that are not loving, more love and joy follow. It is selfish in the best possible way as many courses of action that will hurt another will also lead you to hurt yourself. Recognising that you are all one, can lead you to seeing the other person as loveable and deserving of love and that is closest to the divine energy of the source God.

From our place in non-physical we are often part of the Wave but can perceive the totality of the wave and we can't begin to tell you the beauty and the wellbeing that it is emitting. It is truly magnificent. We have love and appreciation for all that you contribute to the whole.

Are loved ones who have passed aware of our earth journey, from the non-physical plane?

Yes, this is very much the case. The channels of communication are still open even though you may not perceive this to be so. It can be true that your loved ones that are in the non- physical state, have infinitely more power and knowledge than you can access on the Earth plane. It is a wise idea to pray to those that passed over. A relationship can be maintained if you both will it. They are often acting behind the scenes as on your behalf. It is easier for them as they are at a higher vibration than you and they have a multitude of wisdom from past lives. They are whole in their being and that is a powerful state. Ask them to focus their intention on you and for help with whatever your intentions are. They are always willing to help even if your relationship was complicated in life.

In death all the complications are transmuted and all that remains from them to you is pure love that is intensified. The intensity happens because their vibration has increased enormously. We cannot emphasise enough how they are standing by and eager to help you. They are powerful allies. Their hand and handiwork may go unseen in your life, but they are acting in the background easing your path. Their love is ever present. Think of them as smoothing the way or sweeping the path in front of you. They never forget you and have so much love for you. Honour your loved ones that have passed over and your ancestors. They have forged the path for you through very hard lives, and they continue to beam their light towards you lighting up your path and easing your way. They are an army of unseen helpers. We urge you not to forget about them #love your ancestors.

What role do the ancestors play in our lives.

The ancestors who are in their proper place in the universe are loving and appreciating you. Like us, they are beaming love to you directly. Your loved ones who have died have the benefit of their whole beings when they die and they are more powerful. They are helping you from their place in non-physical realms. You can pray to them for help, and it can be possible to feel their presence.

CHAPTER 13

Karma and justice from an angelic perspective

Is justice important in the non-physical realm like it is on Earth. To put it into context, sometimes life does not seem fair to some people. In the example of a child that is suffering or has died where is the fairness in that outcome?

We urge you to not to get involved in the speculation around what is and what is not just, especially not in other people's lives. You cannot possibly know what variables are at play in these situations. There are the issues of past lives, spiritual contracts and karma that will have been agreed to When the soul agrees to incarnate again there are contracts to cover the major life events. You can have no way of knowing what they entail or what was agreed. You also have no sense of what it feels like to be in that person's body and mind and thus you cannot make any assumptions. It is not your business to project your beliefs onto the situation. It is best to hold that person in your mind's eye as being in their strongest state of wellbeing.

When you do not have a full picture of the souls' full being or their past lives you cannot have a true picture of why they came back to Earth and what lessons they are here to learn. It will be too difficult to make sense of and yet we say there is a plan in operation even if does not look like that. For this reason, it is best not to draw too many conclusions from what you observe in the lives of others. If they need help, then you can certainly offer it.

When it comes to the life span of the child, this is agreed as a contract by the incoming soul before they come to Earth. There is purpose in every life no matter how short. You cannot possibly know what their intention was when they came back to Earth. What you may see as a tragedy we see as the fulfilling of that contract and the expansion of that soul and those around them.

We wish to say stay in your own lane and do not project your beliefs onto others. In each lifetime there is plenty to be introspective about and tease out for your own learning, growth and expansion. Therefore, sticking in your own lane is a very smart move.

What of technological advances such as AI and what they mean for humanity.

This is an excellent question. Many of these technologies were born out of a sense of lack and powerlessness of the individual human. They are examples of humans not recognising their inner power and designating their power to an outside source. In fact, humanity has the knowledge to solve all problems that threaten this Earth without seeking help from outside themselves. The answers are within. All wisdom is within because of the mechanism of your higher being who has the benefit and knowledge of all your past lifetimes.

Notwithstanding this, these systems and leaps in technological advances have been brought about by a strong desire to solve problems. For this reason, they may prove to be helpful in some situations. We have spoken to you about intention before, and the intentions of those bringing these technologies into being are most important to consider. Most were built for profit and not for the enhancement of the common good. This can skew how they will develop in the future and often influences the ethical decisions made about their use. When there is corruption and greed as base motivations for a project this tends to taint the overall outcome, which is where we currently are in time. It remains to be seen whether these technologies lead to the advancement of conditions on your planet or not.

In more general terms, there have been many technological advancements such as the internet that have been hugely helpful in the dissemination of knowledge to most people on the planet. Initially there was a broader parity in the accessing of information that would have been the preserves of the very learned and the highly trained in prior times. This rapidly accessible knowledge brought power to the regular person and helped them to be informed. It opened many avenues educationally and for the expansion of the mind as it was easy to access information instantly on any topic that you may have been curious about. It is the accuracy of the information being accessed that is at the nub of the issue. It is important to be discerning when accessing information via the internet. It has always been an issue but now we see a massive intensification of the deliberate campaigns to spread misinformation with covert agendas at play. These campaigns have been successful to an extent that is not fully appreciated by humans at this time, and they have and will play a significant role in how events have played out and will play out in the future. We urge you to be discerning about any information that you read online and question possible agendas at play.

While we do not mean to sound pessimistic the power to influence much of the population of the world is in the grasp of very few individuals. They have no incentive to change the status quo as it benefits them directly. They have a direct platform via smartphones and internet to influence and misinform. They are more powerful than governments and nations now. This imbalance will need to be readjusted if there is to be progress. Rest assured there are the disrupters and agitators who are working against these forces.

What role does Karma play in our current life experience and on past lives?

Karma does exist and it plays itself out over your lifetimes on Earth. It is a complex system that would be impossible for you to totally understand in your physical body. It is not as simple as if you do something bad to someone that you will get your comeuppance at another stage. It is run more on a system of what experiences a soul needs to learn, the lessons that contribute to the evolution of their soul. This is achieved over multiple lifetimes. Sometimes the learning goals are achieved in this life and sometimes they are not and so they will have to be learnt in another lifetime. It is important to know that you agree to re-enter the physical plane time and time again because you have lessons to learn.

It is true that karmic patterns and past lives can cause illness in current lifetimes.

We see this as accounting for a very small proportion of the illness that is occurring in the world now. There is really very little you can do about this, although there are some teachers and therapists who can help work on karma and past lifetimes.

Perhaps the greatest factors and one that broadly goes unacknowledged is the emotional causes of illness. Unacknowledged and suppressed emotion holds an energetic space in the body. If they are continually resisted, they can make a play to be acknowledged. This can often be an illness. We would say you can reduce your chances of emotions causing drama in your body by acknowledging them at the earliest opportunity and feeling them. Many humans fear that if they bring their attention to emotional issues, it will overwhelm them, and they won't be able to cope. The truth is the opposite to this in that bringing attention to these long-ignored emotions can help them to clear. It can feel in the initial phases as if you will be overcome but if you keep your attention on your breathing and the area of your body that is affected you will after a short time feel a shift in the energy of the emotion. It can also be helpful to dip in and out of the process if it becomes too hard. Each time you go back again you are building more resilience towards really engaging with your emotions. It is an ongoing process. By tackling this in small increments it works to clear long buried emotions, and you will also become better at feeling emotions when they initially occur which can transmute them also.

The mental causes of illness are often issues such as negative self-talk, self-hatred and worrying excessively. These patterns become established, and law of attraction brings more of the same. In the case of some illness where the immune system attacks the body's own tissues hatred and disgust directed towards the self are at play. This is known by the medical community who label them auto immune conditions. They cannot really account for how the body attacks itself, but we would say in any cases negative mental patterns are at play.

It is also a truth that the body is designed to last for a long time and to heal itself. This is why there are programmes running continuously while you sleep to upgrade your body through the production of new cells and tissues. The old and damaged cells are destroyed as a protection mechanism. There is great airtime given to lifestyle choices in the determinants of ill health. Of course, this is a factor but not as comprehensively as touted. It does make sense to treat your body lovingly and with respect. Eating nourishing foods and taking exercise is very important.

We mentioned meta-physical earlier, this relates to agreements and soul contracts that you had in place before you reincarnated into your current body. The broad overview of your current life was shown to you, and you agreed to come forth into the physical world and to begin to play your role in the process of creating and expansion. We would like to say that your life is not predetermined. Your personal choice is dominant, and you have full choice in your life. The broad overview you are given at the time of incarnation in mostly in relation to parents, geographical location and some key events that will occur but there is free will and no set pattern or life path is given. Your higher being knows what soul path you have chosen and so takes a broader view of where you are going in life. There may have been illnesses that you agreed to, in your soul contract which may help with growth. It is not possible to know this from your current perspective in the physical world.

So, you can see that the development of illness has multiple determinants many of which you will have little control over while in your physical body. There is significance that you can't always understand. Often the illness you develop is symbolic when you relate it to a mental or emotional pattern that you were operating from. It deserves contemplation in a way that asks what is the body trying to tell you?

As a final word we wish to portray the determinants that impact on the development of disease. We never in any way want to portray that you are to blame for an illness that happened to you. Blame is damaging in any cases as it lowers your vibration. Our intention in answering this question was to make you aware of the many factors that are involved. It is our wish that you may begin to see patterns in your life that may be enlightening. When you bring your attention to something you can begin to change it and, in many cases, gain insight that can guide you in your life.

What is it like to die?

We have told you previously that we are with you at the time of your death and while you are passing between the worlds to your proper place in the universe. There are as many experiences of death as there are people on your planet. This is because of the individual nature of every person and their life experience. There are however factors that are common in the death experience. When you move from the world of matter to the world of higher vibration there is a general experience of expansion. The letting go of the physical shell can mean your vibration changes to encompass senses and knowledge that you could not have previously integrated on the physical plane. Thus comes a greater understanding of your life and life events which is usually reviewed in the moments after death. This process is to integrate the impact of your soul journey to earth on you and other people in your life. All is recorded in the akashic records in any case. Always you can perceive the energy of a previously incarnated being who was significant in your life when you cross over to non-physical.

We do not want to go into detail of the dimension or plane your soul will dwell in after death as it is not possible for you to integrate that knowledge while you are in human form. We do know that there is no death because death is not the end of your journey. When you die your energy rejoins the energy of your higher being which results in a completion of your being. You are most powerful in this form as you are complete and the sum of all the lives you lived and the wisdom you have attained.

The theme of multiple universes where events take place simultaneously across many dimensions at the same time has become well known to humans. We say this is a good way to explain how past lives and reincarnation works. It is however not a complete picture. When you understand that you have had many lives on this planet you begin to see your life and life circumstances from a more impersonal viewpoint. Throughout your different lifetimes you are like an actor, playing out different circumstances mostly with the same souls from previous lifetimes. There may be karma from previous lifetimes that is playing out in your current relationships. If you can imagine the nature of reincarnation, you can detach a little bit from the current reality of your life where everything can seem very personal. The more you personalise things, the more painful they can seem. From a broader perspective adopting this non personal viewpoint and detaching from the circumstances of your current life can allow you to see that you are a powerful soul having a human experience on this Earth. Your intention in coming here was learning and the expansion of your soul and the whole of the universe.

Describing the moment of your passing is not possible because it is individual to every person on the planet who dies. If there is fear around death work hard to reduce this now while you are alive, and death is not imminent. We have told you that death is not an ending. Becoming comfortable with the inevitability of your death may seem like a morbid concept to some. We say it is not, for keeping the impermanent nature of life in your mind can help you to life more fully in the moment.

You have gained glimpses of the afterlife in your highest moments on earth. Those moments when time seems to stand still when you are struck by the beauty of nature for example. Those that meditate will have experience of the time when a blissful feeling of expansion sets in. That experience where you can no longer feel your body and you are weightless and floating. This is why we recommend meditation not just for the raising of your vibration but for the sheer bliss of the experience. Meditating is like dying before you die, a truth the great mystics knew.

Is there punishment in the afterlife if you have made mistakes in this one.

There is not punishment in your sense of the word. A life review is conducted immediately, and you will get a sense of how your life impacted others. There is no judgement whether this was negatively or positively. Your life review serves as a learning exercise. If there are some lessons that you need to learn, these are emphasised for your next incarnation. Always until this review, when you are in your full complete beingness, it is impossible to fully appreciate the impact that you have had on the lives of others. It is a common theme that the soul who is returning to non-physical is often unaware of the profound impacts they have had on others, often changing the whole path of life of another. The life review is not presented in terms of good and bad as humans imagine they will be judged by a harsh God. This is a very one-dimensional way of weighing up a life. It is instead undertaken to learn the lessons of the life that has ended and the expansion of the soul and the addition to greater consciousness of the whole. Those who have led destructive lives and committed heinous crimes according to those of you who would judge, also contribute to the expansion of the whole. This is because they create desires and actions in opposition that lead to growth and expansion. If you think this unjust see our answer to the question on karma.

The concept of justice is an earthly one and does not apply in other planes of existence. The concept relies on the one who judges to be without any deficit of character or besmirchment. (We do not want to say sin as we never want to label any magnificent soul as a sinner). If this was the criteria to be a judge, then there would be no one on Earth who could fulfil it. The futility of judging another when not being capable of comprehending their beingness in the world is staggering from our point of view. It is an impossible task and not one that even God/Source Creator would undertake. This is because all judgement is futile. The concept is deeply flawed.

There is inbuilt mechanism in the human that can be activated when they act outside their values which can be referred to as the conscience. Remorse and guilt can take a heavy toll on the individual. We say there is a natural mechanism at play there. In time all souls will have a deeper understanding of their actions as described above. We want to address those who others would label as psychopaths about whom it has been said they feel no remorse. We say they are better at burying these feelings than the general population, but really, they are delaying the inevitable as they will have to deal with it doubly in the future. There is no escaping from this. It is a law.

There are those who would be angry at what you have said. Perhaps those who have crimes perpetrated on them or their loved ones would be among them. What do you say to them?

This can be a difficult concept to integrate when your society is constantly judging everything and everyone and putting them into piles of wrong and right, good or bad. This is ingrained from a very early age and at every level of society, The whole education system and systems of government and judiciary support these basic concepts of good and bad. We completely understand that the victim of a crime would demand justice. We do not dispute this in any way. A person who committed a violent crime may already be suffering immensely before the crime was perpetrated and afterwards. It may be entirely appropriate that a violent person be rendered incapable of further harming anyone else through incarceration. However, we say that the situation is nuanced. The holding on to resentment by the victim or the victim family is harmful for as long it occurs, which can be decades or carried into the next life. It is energy that is damaging to the person experiencing it and in no way affects the person it is directed towards.

We also feel it is possible to rehabilitate many offenders that may then go on to lead a productive life in society. Redemption is possible always when the person chooses it.

CHAPTER 14

Current world challenges that can affect your Vibration

Is it selfish to focus on what I want when there are so many going through hardship and pain in the world now?

It is true that you see that there is negativity and suffering in the world right now. We however see your world as predominantly one of wellbeing. It is true that we look at it from a perspective of expansion, and the rate of expansion is unprecedented and magnificent to us. It is important to always focus on your vibration first and foremost. You can help others best when you are alignment with the whole of your being including your higher being. It does not help the other to sympathise or feel sorry for them as this is seeing them as less than they are and your sympathy is not as high a vibration as the general wish to uplift them. It is best to see your friend as a being with infinite potential. Hold that vison for your friend, who cannot do that for themselves at that time. That is how you will empower them towards wellbeing because you are coming from the place of your power.

The only possible way that you can have your life be exactly the way that you want it to be is to hold to your vision and consistently flow energy towards it. If you are too preoccupied with the current reality or the negativity that a situation brings then you are less likely to focus what you want into being which includes wellness for your friend. This does not preclude you from helping them in any way you see fit, but you are best served by maintaining your own vibration and then intending wellbeing for them. In this regard putting your own oxygen mask on first or caring about your own vibration is most important.

How can acts of genocide be carried out by seemingly "normal" people?

This is something humans have struggled to understand since the beginning of time. Fear and suspicion of the other can lead to othering of the person or group of people. This fear comes from a basic survival instinct and the fear of being exterminated. It is the basest level fear and very powerful as a result. In this state of anguish, ultimate annihilation of the self is perceived to be a constant threat. The belief that death is the complete end of existence also plays into the fear of annihilation. From this viewpoint any action is justifiable to preserve the body and the life within. No act, no matter how depraved is outside the boundary. It is possible for all humans to reach this state of being through wrong thinking and perception. There are those in powerful positions in this world that know this to be the case, and they act to stoke this fear and suspicion in the full knowledge of how it will play out.

In the current climate it seems very difficult to be hopeful about the future of the world. Is there reason to be hopeful?

Yes of course this is certainly the case. At present you are living in a time of extreme polarity, and it seems there is very little solidarity coming to the fore. We spoke of the news cycle which perpetuates the lie that there is only bad news and nothing to balance that out. From our perspective in the realm of non-physical there is an abundance of wellbeing in this world. We see this in terms of vibration and the vibration of all of humanity or the collective consciousness. It is true that all sentient beings are connected, or all is one. We see the consciousness of individuals rising very fast over a short space of time. The new human beings that are coming into the world are starting at a much higher vibration with a steely resistance not to descend from this to fit in and please others. For the older generations levels of vibration or consciousness is rising too and huge shifts are occurring. This is happening at an unprecedented scale. We can see this on the scale of the whole. Like a grid of lights that are expanding at a level never seen before. We wish that you could see this grid because it looks so beautiful to us. We hold and keep the truth that love is the basis of your universe, and it is abounding and abundant on Earth. We also know that your planet is expanding vibrationally and that expansion is the most important principle of the universe.

Expansion occurs often in reaction to contrasting experiences and that is why it is true that the world is in a time of extreme contrast currently. The division now is part of the process of expansion that will lead to increasing numbers of humans putting out their desires into the world which in turn will lead to changes for the better.

For those of us ill at ease at the disturbing events going on in the world now how can we proceed?

We say take your attention of them for now because you being down about them does not serve the greater consciousness of the world. This is not to say that if you are able to help then you can do so. It is important to consider what is your dominant vibration when you go to help. If you are operating out of a sense of pity for the other this is much less powerful than acting out of a sense of wanting to uplift the person. In this as in all things your intention is important.

If you are in a state of depression and despair about a certain issue, then it is probably best not to act until you can raise your vibration to a higher place about it. We say it is best to take your attention off the greater issues of the world over which you have no control, as your discouragement and despair negatively affect the global consciousness.

We would like also to say that we can see enormous wellbeing in the world that you live in. We can see the planet from a broader perspective, and we are appreciative of all that you and humans in general contribute to the expansion of the universe. We see it from a perspective of growth and so we are not concerned. That is not to say we don't acknowledge that there are people in terrible circumstances in your world.

We say the most important thing is how you feel, and it is important to keep your vibration high as this is contributing to the whole of the collective unconscious. Also, you can be an uplifter for those around you when you keep your vibration high. Do your best to maintain this. We recommend meditation daily or as often as you can. The best time for a meditation is first thing in the morning before there is momentum on other thoughts.

It is important to ask yourself what influence you are operating under. This is crucial to what you will manifest. When your attention is focused in different directions your personal power is split. We are going to say this in a way we never have before. Focus is power for what you focus on brings more of the same. Focusing energy on what you wish to attract then is very important, when trying to bring in more of what you desire.

Your personal power is in the present moment so worrying about the future is just another way of diluting that power. Keeping your vibration high through meditation, intention and focusing on what you desire are powerful ways to manifest the world you desire whether in the personal sense or the example of the world at large.

What is one thing I can do to help humanity and save the planet?

We would say being more selfish by caring how you feel is one of the most important things you can do. Caring about how you feel means keeping track of your vibration and working to keep it high. This means keeping your attention off those things that will certainly lower it such as the news cycle. The reason this is important is because you can become an uplifter of others through your high vibration. Also, you are adding to the whole of the collective consciousness so keeping your vibration high detracts from the mass negativity that humanity is currently experiencing. It also allows you to keep yourself open for inspiration and allows you to change your life.

We recognise that contrasting feelings are often present and that is ok too. When you come to the place where you welcome the good and negative experience equally you will have reached a point of acceptance and allowance. Some would say surrender though this can be off-putting to some. Trying to figure out how to be in a state of surrender when not in one can also be highly stressful. Accept where you are now and go from there.

Sending out positive thoughts and blessings to others can also be helpful. We would say praying but we know some have resistance to this. It is the same thing in any case. As you are all vibration and existing in the mesh of life you can affect another through sending love and blessings. You don't need to know how this mechanism works but know it does. It is of course beneficial to take practical steps to help those in need whether through action or donations of money or time. Remember your intention while doing this is important and so intend to bless all involved and that you will find the best possible action to take.

Mother Earth

We see a planet that abounds with wellbeing and is thriving. The total of your energetic desires for the world has been added to an energetic container and from our position this looks amazing. It is important to know, that for everything that is less than positive on Earth, there are powerful manifesters such as yourself, intending the wellbeing of the planet. In this way, you are contributing to the energetic future of the earth which has not yet manifested. Therefore, we say it is important to pray or intend wellbeing for your planet as you have been doing in greater numbers. It can also be useful to call on the archangels to bless and protect your planet. It is important to see the wellbeing that abounds on this planet also. Being grateful and caring for mother nature is essential because this energy expands outwards to the universe and must in time produce more positive outcomes.

CHAPTER 15

Applying angelic guidance to your life, your life purpose and self-development

What is my highest personal responsibility?

Your highest personal responsibility is to maintain your alignment with your higher being and with source. The good news is this means you should care about how you feel. The reason you are feeling negative emotion is that how you feel about something is indirect opposition to how you higher being feels about it. It is that disconnect that is the source of your discomfort and pain. This is the opposite of what most people do, which is to blame others and situations for their negative feelings. There is absolutely no situation that you could not feel better in by maintaining your focus on what you want and not the situation. You can gradually start to feel better by reassuring yourself and being easy with yourself. All experiences are leading towards your and the universes expansion.

As much as you may desire it, it is not possible to always maintain alignment. This is not something you would want because contrasting experiences are helpful for growth and expansion. Many teachers of the law of attraction say that you create your own reality. We feel that it is more of a co-creation process which we have described before. The key point is that what you focus on you get more of the same from the universe. Like attracts like and this is an irrefutable law of the universe. Once understood it can be hugely helpful is looking at the patterns that are occurring in your life.

What is my purpose here on Earth?

This is indeed a good question and one of the most common that we encounter. You came here to experience all of life and discern what you would like and to create it. You do this through the processes described above by sorting through your experience to decide what you want to create. This is the purpose of negativity and periods of hardship in your life. If you never had these experiences, you could never decide what you do want and desire. On most topics and emotions, you have opposing sides of a coin on which you dwell. When you are on one side you can't experience the other. For example, you cannot experience depression and joy at the same time. It is always a helpful question to ask yourself what side of the coin you are currently on and move towards what you would desire instead. Do bear in mind that momentum can play a role when moving up the scale of emotion. The momentum you have accumulated on any subject can keep you stuck where you may not want to be.

You come here with free will to create a life that is joyful and fulfilling for you. Because there is so much variety in this world, this needs to be decided by you individually. It can be annoying to hear that you can create a life that is joyful and fulfilling to you, especially if you have negative momentum going now. We never mention this truth to condemn you for not being where you want to be. This is never to blame only that you would realise your power to create everything that you desire in your life. We want you to know that you have asked for it and you have created it vibrationally, and it is waiting for you. This is not said to frustrate you, but rather to signpost you on your journey of creation. There is never any blame we rather see you on one side of the coin or having built up momentum on a topic that does not serve you. We know that you can change your mind, and this can change the course of your life. We wait patiently for you to come in the direction of what you want all the while holding you in love and appreciation.

I want to know and carry out my purpose? I am scared about getting it wrong or taking a wrong path?

As we have said before do not worry about getting things wrong it is not possible. We would say your soul has many purposes and it fulfils these across many lifetimes. We have spoken about time not being linear and so you have more time than you think. There is nobody measuring your progress except for you. We know it will all be achieved in divine timing or not at all. Either way it is ok. Be at ease and allow yourself to be as you are and fully accept it. You can only make progress when you fully accept where you are now. It is all working out for you right now in this moment.

I have low energy and am frustrated as there is much I would like to do. How can I proceed?

When you are in a state of low energy it can be a sign that you are stuck in a pattern of low vibrational emotions such as depression. We have discussed in detail that what is likened to itself is drawn in other words your predominant emotion draws more of it to itself. This can explain the feeling of being stuck and low energy.

This is something that you can change gradually because momentum has brought you in one direction. It can take time to move towards a higher frequency vibration. You can do it step by step by prioritizing how you feel and reaching for any good feeling thoughts that you can find. It is our promise if you can stay focused on a positive thought for a short period of time momentum will catch hold of it and expand it.

Being frustrated in the present moment is very understandable. It is important to first work to accept where you are at in the scale of emotions. Frustration can be a helpful emotion when it comes to motivating you because there is energy in it. If you can refocus the energy from blaming yourself towards making some changes this can be helpful.

There are not enough hours in the day. I am so busy and overwhelmed I have forgotten how to feel joy. Can you help me?

Overwhelm is a key indicator that you are not allowing joy and all you have accumulated to flow to you. It is a sign that resistance to the flow of life has taken over. You have dug in so deeply and want to be right so badly that you can't lift your head to see all the good that surrounds you. If we take the analogy of the hole that you are digging for yourself. You are so intent in digging in that you go deeper and deeper. There could be a hand reaching down to pull you out, but you would never see it, so intent and focused are you on the hole in front of you. We have spoken at length about how what you focus on expands. The universe sends you more of what you are currently experiencing. It responds to the vibration of your being.

When you are in the emotion of overwhelm it is often difficult to see the wood for the trees. There are so many thoughts and distractions that it seems like you are powerless. Indeed, in that state the resistance is high, and it is very difficult to get momentum going in any one direction. The fastest way to change direction in terms of momentum is to first accept where you are at and forgive yourself. After that it may be helpful to find some more general thoughts or something to appreciate. It could be the breeze in your hair or the sun on your skin for example. Keeping focused on any one good thing for a while will help momentum to accumulate and gradually you will move towards better feeling thoughts and emotions which will eventually bring you out of resistance. It is a process because changing momentum can take time.

A process that may help is to make a list of all the things that you may need to achieve in any given day. Even the writing of the lists gives you clarity, and it allows you to focus. You can ask for help from the universe to get what needs to be done sorted. A book Audrey appreciated is *Ask and it is Given (2012)* in which the author Ester Hicks channels guidance from her guides Abraham. In this book Ester describes this as the placemat process. When she wrote a list of things that needed to be achieved in the day she was overwhelmed. She assigned some tasks to the universe, and she was surprised to get phone calls and emails about the items she had written down without any action on her part. It may seem to that she had done nothing from an action point of view. On the contrary, what she had done was to come into alignment and intended that the universe would assist her in the achievement of her goals. This was not a passive action, her aligned intention this set into motion the actions that would achieve the task. Just because she was not taking direct action did not mean that she was not responsible. The power of coming into alignment and intending has infinitely more power than the action of doing. This is the key message of this segment. Things that you desire can be achieved easily without struggle and stress on your part when you follow this process. You are much more powerful that you have given yourself credit for.

Is there one pattern that is keeping me stuck?

The most common one is that is unworthiness, blame and shame. These are lower vibrations that can halt your progression in so many ways. When you are feeling stuck in these emotions you are keeping up your umbrella against all the good you already created. This is because your vibration is lowered and because you are not feeling deserving. Your expectation is thus lowered, and it becomes a self-perpetuating cycle. The law of attraction will draw to you more people and events that are of a similar vibration to you and so you would continue to attract negatively while you are in this vibration. The only solution is to break the cycle and raise your vibration which can take time and effort because of the negative momentum that you already have going on. The first step in any change is to accept where you are.

Things are not going my way today. It is one thing after another, and it seems to be getting worse. What can I do?

It can be a good idea to just allow the fact that things have gone in one direction. Resisting reality by blaming or fighting against it will only prolong the misery. Once you have accepted it, please realise that you have momentum built up on the topic and it may take some time to subside. A natural break in these circumstances will follow by going to sleep or taking a nap. It is however important not to reactivate these thought processes again when you wake up, so you do not continue to manifest what you do not want.

I *have low self-esteem, and my life is not going as I hoped it would. What can I do now?*

The aim is to change your vibration. It can take time to become proficient at meditating so be gentle with yourself and allow yourself time, about 15-20 minutes a day. If you need to use music or opt for a guided meditation this is fine. You can begin today to meditate, making a start is most important.

Intending is a very powerful and this is something we have spoken about. Appreciation and acceptance for where you are at this moment will take you far. Small changes can make a huge difference about how you feel about yourself. Give yourself time to try all these suggestions.

Momentum can have a huge impact on your situation as it may not be possible to go from having self-esteem issues to being totally confident overnight. This is because you had a certain amount of momentum going on the low self-esteem beliefs. You can begin to speak to yourself in a gentle way with such reassuring sentences such as, I am doing ok, I am getting better at focusing on what I want. Things are looking up for me. I am a powerful creator. Writing these statements down triples the strength of them and can be very helpful in shifting old beliefs.

Saying and writing affirmations can have a positive effect on raising your vibration. You can write your own. Work on areas on where you have resistance. For example, if you are feeling not worthy you can write I am worthy to receive all my good, I am ready to receive. Everything that you resist can persist and so using affirmations can shift momentum to move you towards the things that you want. See appendix for more affirmations.

Self-development with the angels

What are the practical implications of using the tips and tricks you have given us in this book?

We wish you to become more aware of your guidance system so you can act in alignment with your higher being. Aligned action or simply the state of alignment is a powerful place to be and works with the power of the universe as opposed to working with just the power of your doing which is much less powerful.

The primary reason we have written this book is to help you know of our existence and the possibility of contacting us. We want you to know what supports you have in the non-physical domain whether you choose to call on them or not. We want you to shift your focus from that of a victim to a powerful force in the world. You have the power to be do and have anything you want when you bring your focus to that which you desire on a consist basis in the expectation of receiving it.

We want to emphasise the playful side of life and urge you not to be so serious about everything. In broad terms your life is working out. You may not be exactly where you want to be but accepting where you are now can be the basis of moving forward. We mean truly accepting it by looking at every bit of resentment and resistance you have built up and letting go as best you can. Forgiveness and letting go are very important in helping you to move closer towards your goals.

We operate within the system of collective consciousness and every person who can make progress with coming into alignment with us or their higher being is raising their vibration. This has a direct effect on collective unconscious. In other words, we too have skin in the game. We are working with humanity to ensure the rising of consciousness so that human beings can exist in the higher dimensions of the universe.

We of course want you to realise your goals too on an individual level which is the real reason behind this book. By using the tricks and tips in this book you can access your inner wisdom which will serve you well on the path towards your greatest good. We ask you to go by how you feel. Do you feel the truth in our words? When you meditate or work with your higher being how do you feel? How do you feel in your body now? Is there any reassurance or solace in our words? These are the questions you must ask yourself. Be led by your heart and the resonance of our words. Let our processes be the proof you are looking for. We will be there in any case whether you choose to believe us or not. We will never leave. We are constantly beaming wellbeing towards you and holding you in such high regard. We will never depart from this stance.

How will I get a picture of where my energy is flowing?

Uplifting another is an energetic exchange, but this does not mean that your energy is taken from you. In most interactions this is not the case because there are reciprocal actions from the other and when their vibration rises so does yours. Of course, there are those who will steal energy from you and it is a good idea to be aware of this. You may feel this on a conscious level depending on how sensitive you are. If you were to think about it, you would know those in your life who are sapping your energy.

Being aware of where your energy is flowing is very important to keeping your vibration high. If you were to write down all the areas your energy is flowing or as we might explain it an energetic map. This is something you could attempt over the course of an hour. If you are visual, it can help to draw a map or grid. Place yourself in the middle with lines out to where your energy is flowing. Write as if in stream of consciousness. Note anything that occurs to you. Ensure a large page to allow for all the things you identify as where your energy is directed. Allow time so you can identify all issues. Do not second guess yourself simply write everything down. You may need up to one hour of time to complete this task. When you are finished put it away and go about your business. There is an example of an energy map in the appendix of this book.

It is crucial to come back to your graph when you have about an hour to spare. Give yourself time to read all the list of areas where your energy is flowing. It is fine to amend it to include extra items that occur to you. The task of the exercise now is to find areas where you no longer want to commit your energy and to energetically detach from them.

For example, if it in relation to a person, perhaps an ex-partner, you can begin by deleting old messages between you. You can block their number. Taking down any prominent pictures on display including this person could be important. Removing their images from your online activity can also be helpful. You can the cut cords energetically with the person as described below which can free up your energy and return it to you.

Is the mapping exercise an extensive undertaking?

It can be but just as easily you can quickly jot down some items on a piece of paper and take immediate steps to free up some energy. For example, old job applications, clearing your email inbox, updating your contact list. It may be as simple as clearing out a drawer in your room. You can take steps immediately or plan to do longer decluttering. All these steps bring energy back to you directly. Clearing old energy allows new energy to flow into your life.

Cutting the Cords with Archangel Michael.

If you have identified a person who would like to detach from because the relationship is toxic or for another reason you can cut the cords between you to free up energy. To cut cords with the help of angels, you can take a moment to go within and focus on your breath. Once your body relaxes try to get a mental picture of the person you want to energetically release from. Imagine them sitting in front of you. Can you notice any cords that join you to the person. These can be from any area of their body to yours. Try to visualize the cords. Are they thick like ropes or flimsier such as light string. Call in Archangel Michael three times and imagine him standing in front of you. See him surrounded in light blue light. Take time to visualize Archangel Michael. Notice that he has a sword in his hand. Ask him to cut the cords between you and the other person. See him lift the sword and slice through the cords. Now ask him to fill any spaces where the cords were attached with white light. You can also call on St Germain and the violet flame to transmute any negative energy and to clear you both. Now take the time to thank Archangel Michael and St. Germain for their help. You can bless the person you released and send them on their way if you feel able to. Sit for a while and remain focused within. See if you can sense any change in your energy.

Energetically detaching from life situations.

Another way to energetically detach is, for example with a course you were thinking of doing, to realise that you are holding space energetically for it. If you decide not to proceed with the course it is important to take the dates from your calendar, alert the facilitators that you are not going and delete emails in relation to said course, so you free up your energy around it.

Another example may be of an entrepreneurial idea that you did not follow through on despite being far along in the process. If you do not plan on proceeding with it in the future it can be a good idea to delete all materials related to this also. Again, you are holding space for your creation that has not come to fruition. You must intentionally detach from it to free up energy for your life. Do this even for jobs that you have previously applied for in the past. In essence all your current and past projects are energetically still being endorsed by you. If they no longer serve you take steps to free up your energy from them.

When things are occupying your mind such as an argument with someone or for example if someone is currently bullying you these can take tremendous amounts of energy to process. Even after you work through the action phase or if the issue has been resolved there are still energetic footprints left behind. It is very important to clear these footprints through cutting cords and deleting any physical evidence of the incident.

Freeing up your sacred energy

Most people do not know that their energy is split into so many different areas so completing the tasks described above can be a major eye opener. It may seem overwhelming when you contemplate where your energy is going especially if there are multiple areas, which would be common for most people. Picking an area and taking small actions can make a big difference. While it may seem overwhelming, you can systematically work through things. Pick an area that seems easy to begin say for example a job you have applied for. Delete all correspondence and written material pertaining to the job. Once completed you can move on with your day and come back to the list the next day. It doesn't have to be difficult. By simply bringing awareness to where your energy is flowing it can be revolutionary as that knowledge gives you the power to change. The result of this process is that you will begin to free up your energy, and you will be more cognisant of where your energy is flowing in the first place. Simply put this is a win-win situation. The most difficult part is just starting.

A lovely benefit of freeing up this energy is that you can come more into alignment with your higher being. Also, you begin to dedicate more energy to focusing on what you want to attract into your life. The energy that is freed up enhances your power of attraction significantly. You will find yourself clearer around where you are willing to expend your energy and better boundaries will ensue. The power of your being will expand exponentially. Your life will begin flow better as a result. In conclusion, we cannot recommend this process enough, get started and we know you will see results.

Forgiving yourself

I am finding it difficult to forgive myself for something I that happened when I was younger. Can you help me?

We have spoken about forgiveness as a process which it very much is. Most humans find it easier to forgive another before forgiving themselves. All healing and reconciliation can only take place in the present moment. The past is gone and there is little to be gained by dwelling there (we do recognise this is a very common pattern though).

It may be that you have deemed yourself responsible for something awful that happened in the past. Firstly, it can be a good idea to examine this closely to see whether there is any truth in the matter at all. For example, many children blame themselves for the death of a loved one even though there may be no truth to this whatsoever. Really look at your part in what you are blaming yourself for. Is this even reasonable or rational? Were there other factors at play beyond your control? Spend a short time doing this. You may be surprised to learn that your perceptions now are very different to then.

Be willing and open to letting yourself off the hook even if you still feel guilty after the above process. A willingness to let go is the most important part of this process. You can't change the past but be willing to allow yourself to think differently about it. If you feel you want to make amends, move forward with this. If you are very stuck around the issue, use the process of writing positive aspects about yourself. This can be difficult. Try to add to the list or at least look at the list every day. The aim of this is to come to the realisation that you are a person who has made mistakes, and you are worthy of receiving compassion from yourself. Self-compassion is very powerful, and it has the power to change completely how you feel about yourself. Be gentle and easy with yourself and know it is a process that will take time

CHAPTER 16

Overcoming relationships Issues with the angels

My relationships are fractious, and it is affecting my life. What can I do?

It is true that nothing that anybody else does need affect you. This is a tricky one for humans to acknowledge as most tend to blame others for their life situations. Looking for your own contribution to any situation will bring you a clearer perspective. As blame is a higher vibration than anger, humans often blame others without taking accountability for their own actions.

It can be helpful to write down and look at your beliefs about the situation from all perspectives. Challenge thoughts that are projections and those that you cannot know for sure are true. Are you holding on to assumptions about the situation that are not true? Are you projecting your feelings onto others when you cannot know how they feel? We would not blame you in any way for situations in your life. We are just pointing out the truth may be more nuanced than you have been able to admit to yourself. It can be impossible to take any learning from a situation when you cast yourself as a victim. Indeed, a victim mentality can make life seem unbearable. Look at the situation rationally and see what learnings can be taken from it. Writing it down is usually the best way to do this.

It may be the case that you were victimised in a situation and that is ok to acknowledge. Your power comes back to you when you decide how you will respond to the situation. It may be that you take steps to confront the other person. It may be that it is wise to avoid that person in the short term. In intimate relationships you can look at a way to present your feelings on the situation in a way that the other person will hear them. You can only be accountable for your own behaviour and if the other is not willing to do the same acknowledge that is where they are at. It does not mean that you need to stay with them or put up with any behaviour that is not loving. Watch your own reactions and take a small pause before you respond. It is fine to take time to listen to your gut and contemplate the next best move.

Ultimately your life is your energy. It is common knowledge that there are people in this world who consciously or unconsciously steal the energy of others. It can be very helpful to take an inventory if there are those people in your life. Unfortunately for some these will be intimate partner, spouses or even children. Knowledge is power and even knowing how others steal your energy can be enlightening without having to act on it. There are strategies to deal with this for some, the best option may be to distance from such a person. This may seem like an uncharitable thing for angels to say after we have described to you how all humans are magnificent in appearance to us. It is not a contradiction. Acceptance of where the person is at that time is the best strategy. It is important to decide for yourself what is acceptable to you in a relationship. We have given you strategies to clear, ground and protect your energy.

I do not have a good history with relationships. I seem to attract the same type of people into my life. They are love bombers and charming in the early days but turn jealous and abusive as time goes on. What can I do?

The essence of this situation is at its core vibration. The patterns and events of your life have caused you to be vibrating at a certain level which attracts partners at a similar vibration. It can be that you create relationships that you have seen in your immediate family. Perhaps, if you had an emotionally unavailable parent, you attract an emotionally unavailable partner. It is possible you agreed to these relationships as a learning device in your soul contract. However, when the same problems reoccur repeatedly and you do not learn from them, that is not progress. You have come to the awareness of this dynamic, which is the first step in remedying it. You correctly believe that you have played a part in the manifestation of the dysfunctional relationships which is indeed is the case. We say this not to blame in any way.

There is a vibrational element at play here, and to attract a different partner you need to change your vibration. It may be that you look at the previous relationships with an open mind being willing to see the instances that you overrode your own innate wisdom and put that person's needs above your own. This is deep work, and you may need the help of a counsellor. Awareness and acceptance of past patterns is the goal, as is learning the lessons you can take from these relationships. Nothing is wasted, as to hone your desire towards what you really want, it was favourable to experience the opposite of that. You have now come to a stronger place of desire to attract the relationship that is satisfying to you. This is why blame is unnecessary.

It is important always to care about how you feel and try to keep positive thought as dominant. It can also be a good idea to make a list of attributes your ideal partner would have. Keep it somewhere you can see it every day. Really spend time creating a mental image of this partner. Dwell on the feeling of excitement and potential of having a new partner in your life. Doing this you are laying the tracks of a new relationship and taking your mind off the temptation to view the world from a sense of lack.

We will say that, without exception, you knew the game of the people you were involved with previously. You knew that there were red flags instantaneously, but you overrode your instinct in continuing in the relationship. You may not have been aware of this on a conscious level, but you were aware. It is important to go within and ask why you have not heeded your own personal warning system and why the outer world takes more of your attention than your inner wisdom. We say this not to blame you in any way only to draw conclusions about what you want in a relationship going forward.

Finally, your past relationships have not been for nothing. They have allowed you to come to a clearer picture of what you want in a person and a relationship. This is not insignificant and is the basis of all creation and so do not look back with regret. Instead look forward for you have created a wonderful relationship vibrationally and it is waiting for you in vibrational form. Just come to a happier place from which it will have to manifest.

I feel trapped in my relationship. My partner does not understand me or my interests and belittles me. What can I do?

We understand that is a difficult situation for you. It may be the case that you have lost some confidence because of your partner's behaviour. From his part this is very much a strategy to keep you small so you will remain in the relationship. Ask yourself how this relationship serves you in your life? Will expansion and growth be possible in this relationship? Can you be your authentic self in this relationship or are you always making compromises or making yourself small?

You and your partner came together when you were a similar vibration and wanted the same things. Your vibration has now risen, and you see your situation more clearly. A loving relationship is one where you are accepted for who you are. A loving partner does not need to demean you or indulge in power struggles. People can drift apart when their vibrations begin to differ, and it is ok to release this relationship now should you feel ready.

A common misconception that humans have is that they can change another person. When you look at it from a vibrational point of view you can see the folly in this because everyone simply is where they are on a vibrational scale. Moving from where you are takes time and effort and so to assume another who may or may not be willing, can be changed is foolhardy. Accepting them as they are now, allows you to decide whether they are compatible with you in the present moment.

We would like to point out that you have power in this situation. You have the insight to know what it is you want. This will already have created more improved relationships in vibrational form. If you decide to release your current partner, you will automatically move towards these manifestations. Begin to see yourself as free and choosing what you would like in your life. Begin to see that you are not stuck and that there is a myriad of opportunities for you to be, do or have what you want.

I have been unable to find a life partner and I would very much like to do so. Can you advise me?

It is important to take your attention of the lack of a partner or what is missing and instead focus on what type of partner you would like to attract into your life. This is because keeping your mind focused on lack just invites more lack into your life. Writing lists of aspects that you would value in a partner can focus your energy. You should be as specific as possible.

When you feel the absence of your partner refocus on the list of positive aspects you have created. Affirmations can be helpful in keeping your vibration high and help you to focus in the direction of what is wanted. Work on feeling good before affirming. Here are some examples.

I am feeling good about myself today.

I have a great personality, and I am a wonderful partner.

New and exciting people are attracted to me now.

I easily discern those who are on the same wavelength as me.

It is all working out beautifully.

These are just examples, and you can create ones that have resonance with you. Writing them down makes them more powerful. Allow yourself to feel excited and positive about the future as this is the first step in attracting someone new into your life. Go over the processes of manifestation detailed in this book.

My partner and I are fighting a lot. What can I do?

This behaviour can carry its own momentum. It can accentuate resentment and anger and add momentum to these feelings leading to worse outcomes. The first action is to accept the situation as it is. Both of you contribute to the dynamic when there is constant fighting. Your partner is as he/she is, as are you and there is disharmony now. Now ask yourself what is it you want? It may be that you have an abusive partner, and you have concluded that you want to leave the relationship without putting yourself in danger. It may be that you realise that you would like to stay in the relationship and are willing to work on yourself and the relationship together as a couple so it can continue. It may be that you have realised that the relationship was over many years ago, but you have been holding on to it out of fear of being alone. It can be any of these circumstances and many others that it is not possible to list here.

First, accept it as it is. When you get to the level of acceptance you can free up energy to move forward how you would like to proceed. When you proceed with clarity it leads to better outcomes for yourself and your partner. In any case, independent of what you decide it can be helpful to write a list of the aspects of your partner that you appreciate. If you put your focus on these aspects it can help to release resistance and help you see the humanity of the other person which means you are less likely to react to the situation. Finally, it is ok to take time to decide what you want. If you can be comfortable in the not knowing and intend clarity things will change.

I am going through a contentious divorce, and I am finding it difficult to forgive my ex. Can you help me come to be at peace with this?

You can intend harmony in your relationship even if you are separating and you can intend that things will work out in the best interests of all concerned especially if there are children involved. Taking time to reflect and be clear on how you wish to move forward is crucial. For example, if being a united front that supports the children is a key value of yours then forging communication and harmony with your soon be to ex-partner is vitally important. A view that many don't consider is that you can influence how it turns out through the power of intention and with a generosity of spirit. Too often in divorce, one person takes a position of victimhood and fear overcomes them and so they react more aggressively to protect themselves. Adopting that position is always one of weakness. We agree that it is difficult and painful to go through divorce, and it triggers your deepest feelings of being threatened. We say be willing to feel this discomfort and take time to come to a clarity about what your key values are in relation to how it will progress. You have power in how the divorce turns out. Use this power by becoming non-reactive, using the power of intention and allowing your ex-partner to be where they are without trying to change them. You can of course defend your interests with lawyers if you so wish but always ask yourself if how you are proceeding is in line with your values.

Forgiveness is a process, and you can often be asking too much of yourself to expect yourself to grant it immediately. If you did that it would not be true forgiveness because you would surely be holding on to resistance and resentment. It takes time to forgive but intending harmony when interacting with your ex-partner is very important. Finally, if you can stay open, curious and loving throughout the whole experience of the divorce you will learn some very useful lessons about yourself. Like all distressing life events there is the possibility of becoming more awakened and authentic.

I have allowed another to disrespect me once and now he continues to bully me. How can I proceed?

It is interesting how you have phrased the question in that you allowed someone to disrespect you. There is certainly an energy of allowing even though it may not be conscious on your part. We again say this not to blame or be in any way controversial but there is always an allowing by the person who is being bullied. Again, this may be totally unconscious. It may stem from a feeling of not feeling good enough or trying to please another. We are aware that these vibrations often come from previous patterns in childhood or social conditioning so there is no blame attached on our part whatsoever. There are those that are very adept at sensing or picking out those people who would not retaliate. It is a vibration between the two that is sustained on both sides. We realise that this may sound distressing to those of you who have been in abusive relationships. Again, here we merely try to explain the intricacies of the interaction.

It is well known that the most effective interaction with a bully is direct confrontation or else the behaviour will not change and in many cases it will intensify. This can also be accomplished through an intermediary or through grievance processes for example. It is essential to do the vibrational work on yourself to alter your predominate vibration that allowed this behaviour of another. Again, there is no blame attached but not recognising this can leave it wide open for the next bully to come along.

My partner has just left me, and I am eaten up with grief and can't function. What should I do?

We absolutely know how difficult this is for you, and we send you love. The first step as always is acceptance of where you are now. This could be a realisation that you can't accept that he is gone. Allow yourself to feel the feelings of sadness and grief in whatever small way you can. It is fine to dip into and out of feelings if they are overwhelming to you. Take some time out from life to come to terms with what has happened. The sooner that you can accept the situation as it is the quicker you open the door to healing.

Your predominant thought pattern in your current situation is focusing on what you have lost and feeling a sense of loss. Momentum will attach to these thoughts and send you more of the same. It can be helpful to move your thought from the specific to the more general and then it may be possible to find some small things to appreciate. By placing your attention on things you appreciate, even for short periods it can allow your vibration to rise incrementally.

If all of this seems too much and you feel stuck or not able to function, then it is best to do nothing and simply allow yourself to be in this state. It is part of a process of healing for you, and it is important to honour it. Allowing yourself to be as you are and not judging yourself or forcing action is the most compassionate thing you can do for yourself. Feeling the feelings associated with this will help you process and release the grief. Do not make any projections into the future such as never being able to find another partner for example. In your current vibration it is not the time to create for the future until you have moved through it. Know that you will move through this stage and begin to feel better soon.

I have been betrayed by my spouse who is having an affair with my friend. It is so painful to be betrayed in such a fashion. I feel it physically in my body like a knife through my heart. How can I go on?

We are with you, and we send you love. This is indeed a very difficult situation. As you mention, many people can feel grief in their bodies that is a manifestation of emotional pain. The pain of betrayal can be intense and there is an element of shock because you had not been expecting this. If you can try and feel the pain as it is, and to sit with the feelings around it. Acceptance is always the first step on the road to recovery.

It may seem to you that you can't trust yourself because you could not have predicted this event. You can and should trust yourself. You are a powerful creator. Where there have been relationships that have been characterised by betrayal, you have created relationships that are loving and trustworthy in vibrational form. While there have been friends who ultimately betrayed you, you have created trustworthy relationships with friends that love and support you. The desire and wanting caused by this betrayal, has set into motion vibrationally wonderful new friendships and circumstances that will be thrilling to you. It may seem like a stretch now, but you can trust in their existence.

Most importantly trust in yourself. You will know what to do and how to move forward. Trust in how you are feeling and know all your feelings are valid. Trust that you will have other loving relationships in your life. Trust in us because we are very much, in conjunction with your own guides, beaming wellbeing towards you. We have seen all the wonderful things you have created in your future, and we are amazed. We can see your brilliance and your wellbeing and are confident that you will come to appreciate these yourself more in time.

I am getting on badly with my boss. What can I do?

We agree that this can be difficult because many of you have convinced yourself that you must stay in the same job and there is no possibility of another job coming ever. We say this not to mock you in any way. The most stressful piece of this dilemma is not the strife at work but rather the thought that there will never be another job opportunity so that you can escape this work hell that you are currently in. We can reassure you that there are always opportunities for those that are clear in their desires and intentions. This is a law of the universe. Nevertheless, you have convinced yourself that there will never be any other opportunities for you.

The first step is to accept where you are at right now. Writing a list even if it is short of the things you appreciate about your current job can be helpful even if it is only the pay and that it is close to home then write that. You may find there are more things than you have thought. Next it is a good idea to write some positive aspects about your boss. Even if it is your intention to leave your job and you feel that you cannot stand your boss this is essential to do. Expect a good deal of resistance to this at first. Think about anything at all. It could be that they are punctual or how they dress or that their work is neat. This may seem counterproductive, but we say it is not. This is because you have built up a great deal of resistance by resenting your situation and your boss and this is taking up a lot of energy. Allowing yourself to appreciate some aspects of your job and your boss frees this up. This energy can be harnessed towards changing the situation.

Once you begin to appreciate some things about your current work situation and free up your energy from resisting and resenting, watch how your experience at work will change. You may move through the day more easily and finding yourself enjoying the work more. Keep focused on the things that you appreciate about your boss for one week and see if the relationship changes at all. Most of the time other people can perceive consciously or unconsciously your thoughts and feelings about them. This can lead to energetic disharmonies and blocks in the energy between you. When you release the resistance (resentment) often the relationship changes and flows more freely. If this is not the case, ask yourself are you still holding on to resentment, because you have given yourself the role of victim, for example. Stay open and curious and be willing to be honest with yourself. Even if nothing changes with the relationship you have freed up energy which can go toward finding a new position.

When you have followed the above process, you are now in a much better position to start to look for another job. The most important thing is to be open to the possibility of limitless opportunities to achieve this goal. It can be helpful to write the details of your ideal job and focus on this while you are intending to attract new work opportunities. Intending daily will move you closer to your goal. Accepting your current job situation is important. When you have an idea of the job you would like to attract and have written about it and intended it then surrender it to the universe and do not be concerned with timelines. Simply let it go. Start applying for any jobs that interest you. Begin to realise that there are infinite opportunities out there. There are as many opportunities as you believe there to be.

Take your mind off any feelings of panic or feeling stuck as this will keep you where you are. Instead look at how you will feel about starting a new job elsewhere. It is important to appreciate yourself also and what you can bring to another job. Simple affirmations such as people are always looking for the skills that I have. I am always in demand. I easily attract more exciting opportunities to me. I am appreciated for my ability and my interpersonal skills. Keep these somewhere you can see them and keep up your vibrational work daily and watch what happens.

CHAPTER 17

Recalibrating Fear to Love

I am worried about my finances. I am just about making ends meet. I worry if prices rise, I won't be able to afford to live. How can I become more abundant?

When you worry about your finances you are placing your attention on the lack of money, and it is this lack which becomes active in your vibration. When the lack of money is predominant the law of attraction brings more lack to this dominant vibration, for example you may have an unforeseen bill. The key is to take your focus off the financial situation and place your attention on anything small that pleases you to shift your vibration.

It can be a good idea to think about what abundance means to you. This can be a useful exercise to complete on paper. Are there ways that you can feel abundant in your daily life? Perhaps treating yourself to something small that makes you feel good. Once you begin to define what abundance means to you, it is helpful to feel the feeling of what it would be like to have this abundance in your life. Thinking about this in detail can be helpful. What would it feel, taste, smell, sound and look like. Give time to really feel the feeling and then release it all to the universe.

We can promise you that the abundance that you desire has been created when you asked for it and is waiting in vibrational form for you. Therefore, working on becoming aligned through meditation and affirmations or positive statements can be helpful. The most important factor is your vibration. Negative and doubting thoughts automatically take you away from this alignment. We know this information will be frustrating to hear but it is true.

It is now a good time to daydream about how attracting more money could change your life. Journalling can be helpful, but the most important part is to feel the feeling of abundance in whatever form it appeals to you. When you take your attention of the current reality and place it on the reality you want to attract your manifesting power multiplies exponentially.

Expectation is a part of this process because what you expect to happen is more likely to come into reality. Conversely you can do all the processes and daydreaming in the world and if you do not feel worthy to receive this can be a block. Affirming this worthiness through affirmations and working through any blocks on this issue will also be effective. This is one thing we don't urge patience on. Take steps to feel as good as possible right now.

I have been comparing myself to others and I fear I come up short in many ways. What can I do?

We wish you could see yourself are we can. We see you as a magnificent creator who is so powerful that you are bending the world to your will. Your gift and talents are unlimited. We can see that you are kind and the myriads of ways that you uplift others in your world. To us, you shine like the brightest star in the sky. You are unique and the only one of you in the entire universe, we have so much love for you.

It has been said that comparison is the thief of joy. We wholeheartedly agree with this assertion. There are so many of you all vibrating at different levels, all focused on what you desire and manifesting a huge variety of things and situations.

It is amazing to us that you would compare yourself to anyone else. You are unique and there can never be a comparison that is accurate.

Therefore, take your mind off this comparing whether that be stopping your thought on it or avoiding social media that is triggering to you. Make a list of positive aspects about yourself and try, every day, to appreciate something. We and your higher being are appreciating you so much. Remember, we are beaming wellbeing towards you from our place in non-physical. If you could get anywhere in the vicinity of this vibrationally you could begin to see yourself as we do. Even if this is not possible you can intend to take your attention off these negative thoughts about yourself. Use all our processes to move vibrationally towards more positive feelings about yourself. You can do this.

I have cancer and I am in such fear and panic right now. *How do I proceed?*

As always, we are with you and sending you love. When fear and panic are the predominant emotions in you experience it is difficult to move forward. It can be overwhelming. In this initial period, it is best to take time to reflect. It is wise to do nothing until the initial wave of fear and panic abates because they are low vibrational states from which you don't want to project into the future.

You have no way of knowing what this experience will bring. Once you have taken the time and if you have decided on treatment options your intention will be very important. Intention is powerful in creating your day-to-day experience and so remember to use it. Intend and surrender the outcome to the universe. You can intend safety and wellbeing while on treatment if this feels right to you.

Present moment awareness can be so powerful when dealing with any big challenge. What can seem overwhelming in outlook can be easily managed in present awareness. Allowing yourself to operate from this point of view can be very helpful. From our perspective everything happens in the present moment. The past is over, and the future is not here yet. All healing happens in the present moment. Cultivating present moment awareness through meditation and mindfulness can be very helpful. Your guides and angels are with you throughout and ask for their help. They will move in ways behind the scenes delivering conditions and people that will be helpful to you. This is our promise.

I am afraid of dying. How can angels comfort me at my time of death?

We have mentioned before that we are with you in your time of transition to the non-physical plane. We are working behind the scenes to make your transition as easy as possible, and we go with you to the next plane too. While in physical form it can be difficult to sense our presence due to the difference in vibration between us. In the moment of your passing, you will feel the full presence of the love and support of your guides, as well as rejoining your higher being and becoming whole. It can be a blissful experience. Soon after you will begin to understand all your experiences of this lifetime, in relation to the learning that resulted from the life you lived. When fear is removed all that is left is the essence of your soul which is pure love.

I am talented creatively and have lots of interesting work under my belt. I am scared to put myself out in the world to promote my work. I have a lot of fear about this. How do I overcome this?

This fear comes from a perception that you are not worthy to receive. In another terms it can be that a part of you is stuck in fear around the thought of exposing yourself to criticism and it is a part that is trying to keep you safe. This part developed in response to life circumstances when you were younger. Go within and reassure this part that you are now older and more capable of dealing with what comes your way.

The other thing to bear in mind is that fear and hope are on different ends of the same scale which means that it is impossible to feel both simultaneously. You can begin to move towards hope by allow momentum to gain traction on positive thoughts. This process has been discussed before in this book. Moving towards more hopeful thought, you can make a list of all your positive aspects. You have already everything you need within you to progress in the direction you need to go.

Once you appreciate yourself and the extent of your personal resources you can move forward. In reality, the fear does not have to be gotten rid of because it was a healthy self-protective mechanism that simply got out of control. It is ok to feel the fear but to move forward anyway. That is our message because it is unrealistic for most, bar the extremely enlightened, to never feel fear. Also, it is not desirable as it has arisen as a protective measure and it still has something to teach you, notably how you integrate it and proceed with your endeavours whole heartedly when it is present.

We see your gifts as an artist and will say that your art has much to offer others in terms of inspiration and bringing comfort to others. We promise you that your work will be meaningful and impactful to others. Accept and feel the fear and overcome it so you can reap the rewards of your hard work.

I feel like time is running out for me and I can't seem to change things. What can I do?

We would begin by saying that the idea that time is running out is indeed a fearful thought and bears no resemblance to reality. We have said before that time is a construct here on Earth and it is not the reality of the universe which is more structured like the multi verses we were taking about earlier. When you have a stressful thought like this you are deepening resistance to things changing in your life. Like in the analogy before, you are digging yourself a hole that is going deeper. The first action as always is to find some general thought that are pleasing in some way to you. This is like lifting your head to see your surroundings when you are in the hole. It is the first step in you getting out of the hole. In other words, taking your focus off the unwanted is the first action.

Once you begin to focus on what you desire for longer periods of time momentum will cause you to move in the direction of what you want. The more time you spend focusing on this the more momentum can add to it and the more powerful your capacity to manifest. Intending daily how you would like your day to unfold is very powerful. Meditation and coming into alignment with your higher being will mean that you are moving more quickly towards the life you desire. Taking you focus off what you don't want and focusing on your desires is important. There are many processes described in this book that will help you create the changes you want to bring about in your life.

I am going through an intense period of depression, and I feel lost and afraid how can I contact you?

You need do nothing as we are there holding you in high regard and beaming our wellbeing towards you. It can feel when you are depressed that you are completely alone and that there is no hope. It is like you are holding up an umbrella and our high vibrations are not reaching you. This is because like goes with like and it may be impossible to reach us when you are at a low vibrational state. We never leave nor ever stop seeing you in your full resplendent glory. We are like besotted parents who can never take their eye off their offspring. There is no disconnect but we are just not on your radar, but you can always turn to us. Ask us for signs, ask us to enfold you in our powerful wings. We are always there. Turn towards us and ask for our help. Audrey hears us by having tuned her radar towards our signal and having reached vibrational equivalence of us. She does not always maintain this, but she does go offline very infrequently these days. Our message is that we are always there and seeing and appreciating your total being. Our love is always directed towards you.

I feel very numb frightened of feeling my feelings. What can I do?

We know that you can become overwhelmed with your feelings. Feeling numb is very much resistance to feeling anything at all but it is also cutting yourself off to the flow of life. We see feelings and emotions as tremendously important in helping you to create the life you desire. We have described how negative feelings bring more of the same via the law of attraction. However, they can also strengthen your desire to have a positive experience. The positive experience is created in vibrational form and will manifest once you move towards it by feeling good. Therefore, emotions positive and negative (we see all emotions as positive), are incredibly important in the process of manifestation.

Allowing emotions to flow through you, knowing they are transient is essential. When you are feeling numb, you are actively blocking feeling any emotion and that can keep you stuck. Can you gradually allow yourself to feel some part of your body that feels safe. This could be your hands; any part of your body is fine. Bring the attention back to the body and it will ground and support you. It can be helpful to imagine your body as a solid container that can hold all your emotions. Audrey sometimes projects this container out to the four walls of the room she is in and imagines them containing her feelings. Another technique is to find where a certain emotion is in the body, for example anger could be in the chest, bring your full attention to this area and feel the intensity of the anger. Even if it is uncomfortable keep your attention focused on it for a few moments. Gradually you will see it will shift and lessen in intensity. It can be helpful to bring the attention to the body to fully experience the emotion because then you can shift and transmute it. This is the basis of all healing.

We spoke of momentum earlier and we know it can take time to go from a place of resisting all emotions by feeling numb and being willing to start to feel these emotions. You may need someone, a professional or a friend, to help and support you in this process, so you feel safe. Any step you can take to shift the momentum will be helpful. A willingness to allow and curiosity is all you need. Be gentle with yourself during this process.

CHAPTER 18

Parenting with the angels

My child is seriously ill. I am paralysed with fear of losing them. I know this is not helpful in helping bring about the best recovery for them. How do I move out of this stage?'

It is first very positive that you have an awareness of the impact of negativity on how things may turn out. This is not in the general population's awareness and so we commend you. It is possible to move to a better feeling vibration, and it is a good idea to do so. Accepting the situation as it is, not as how you would like it to be, is the first action. It will also be wise to acknowledge that in many ways you do not have control over the situation. We know this is terrifying to you, but it is the truth. You can control your own vibration through the work we have been describing It is a good idea to do so as it will be uplifting for yourself and your child. It may not be possible to find positive aspects of your child's situation and we would urge you to put your attention on a different topic. It may be a good feeling place in your body or for example that the flowers in the room look beautiful. Allow yourself to bring more focus and expansion to the good feelings and thoughts. It is impossible to feel fearful and hopeful at the same time so as you begin to rise your vibration towards more positive emotions your attention naturally falls away from the vibration of fear. The more attention you can place of the positive momentum will take hold of it and expand these feelings.

We will say that you cannot know why this situation has manifested in your child's life. We cannot know about their soul contract or karma from other lifetimes that may have meant that illness would show up in their experience. Therefore, do not apportion blame especially to yourself. This was not created by you, so it is a false narrative to blame yourself. It also takes your attention away from the reality of the present moment. There will be opportunities for becoming closer to your child in the time you spend together in the hospital.

The emotion of terror is one that can elicit a feeling of paralysis, very much like a deer in the headlights you can become frozen. Movement of any kind can help with this be it stretching or any other form of movement. Often you see anxious people pacing as it brings relief from that feeling of paralysis. It is a process to move towards more positive emotions so give yourself time and be patient with yourself. The fear may creep back in and that is to be expected. We want you to know that in any given moment you have power over your own vibration and how you react to any situation.

Of course, it is beneficial to pray for your child and intend safety for them. Having intentions too can be very important in shaping how the day goes. Focusing on the positive aspects of your child can help them too. This is because you are seeing their strengths and appreciating them in the moment. All vibrational work you do on yourself and on your relationship with your child will have rewards.

I have been in caring roles my whole life and have noticed that my wealth and opportunities have been affected by prioritizing others over myself. How can I move through this?

We understand that it feels like you have put others before yourself. You have also told yourself the story that because you have prioritised caring for others your life has been negatively affected. We say you cannot know this is true. It may be true that you may not have earned as much financially, however there are many benefits of caring for others, and few would deny that it can feed the carer also, who certainly gains from the interaction. The satisfaction of being happy in your work cannot be underestimated. Therefore, you may not be acknowledging the need you had to act in the role of carer but also the payoff from the caring interactions which can add to the sense of purpose in your life. Look honestly at how you feel about your current caring roles. If you are not happy, you can change things. You do not have to continue in any roles that you no longer wish to fulfil. We have spoken a few pages ago about putting other's needs above your own so re read that answer. Only you can decide what you prioritize in your life but by looking honestly you can accept where you are and begin to make changes should you so wish.

I am worried I will get things wrong raising my children. I feel like any mistake could be detrimental. I want to do better as a parent what should I do?

We want to firstly point out that like you, your children are magnificent creators of what they desire, and they have come here under similar conditions to create conditions that are pleasing to them. They too, as are all in your world are governed by the law of attraction. The new ones that are coming in the last twenty years, have even greater manifestation power and they will not tolerate conditions that are unsatisfactory, and so they are even more effective creators.

When you realise that your children are individuals that have come to create their own reality, you can appreciate that you are not, nor could you ever be, responsible for their experience in this world. They will make their own mistakes, as you have done, but by doing so will bring about the conditions through their desires and what they allow; to have life exactly as they would like it. Adversity or contrast may be necessary to increase desire and thus manifestation power. This is the natural way of the world. You cannot know what soul contracts or karmic agreements they have. Self-blame is futile and we see it as quite arrogant because you do not have the power to override the conditions from which they are attracting. Release this instantaneously because it is a falsehood and a distraction from getting closer to the truth. Bearing all this in mind both you and your children will make mistakes which are necessary to enhance your power to manifest.

There are certainly things you can do to support your children notwithstanding providing them with food, shelter, education and love. The first is accepting and allowing them to be who they are. They have come to be their own magnificent creators and so you must look at any ways you are trying to shape them or mould them to your will and stop this behaviour because it is futile and damaging to the essence of your child's being. As described before you can write positive aspects of your child and focus on these regularly. Focusing on the positives expands these and the positive energy flowing between you. You can also pray for your children and use the power of your intention to put powerful suggestions out to the universe as to what they might attract. Keep these general, such as safety, abundance and harmony because you cannot dictate specific conditions for them. Ignoring negative attributes is important, as by placing attention on these, disharmony between you can grow. This is not to say that you can't put boundaries in place with your child. These are essential for a sense of safety for your child. Punishment for perceived bad behaviour never works because it places attention on the negative which means more negative behaviour will ensue. Asking the question of what is behind the behaviour and dealing compassionately with your child will mean that the relationship between you remains strong.

Finally, when you see your children as they are, creators and powerful individuals, the relationship becomes one of equals and you open the space for you to learn from your children. You own soul contract has allowed them to come into existence for your learning, expansion and enlightenment. There is much to learn on both sides.

I have teenagers and I am challenged by them daily. I feel like they are pushing my buttons, I am trying not to react. Can you advise me?

It is a truth that your children are sent to help you become more conscious by drawing attention to your wounds, they help you to evolve if you are willing. On a soul level, in your soul contracts, you both agreed to incarnate at this time together to teach each other lessons and to evolve. If you can understand that your children are here to help you evolve and process your wounds because they are as enlightened as you. In most cases they are more so. This can be a chilling thought for your ego.

Connection is crucial

The traditional parenting model of authority where the parent supposedly knows best and imposes their will on the child needs to be left in the past. Parenting from an egoic perspective causes you to constantly identify perceived flaws in your child and implement punishments for transgressions. What suffers most in this model is the connection between parent and child the very cornerstone of the relationship. Your child begins to withdraw gradually from you. It can be very painful for a child to perceive that a parent does not understand them at all.

It is a good aim to put connection at the heart of parenting. In this way, you can always prioritise the bond between you. You can look to your child to show you what they are interested in and follow their lead. There are times your children will make mistakes, but parenting that prioritises the bond while challenging the behaviour is crucial.

We understand that parenting is difficult, and we are sympathetic. Ask yourself are you projecting your own worries and insecurities on to your child? Are you pushing them to achieve in academia and sports to satisfy your own ego? By looking at your own motivation, you will spare your child feeling like they are only the sum of their achievements. This sends the signal that they are not loved unconditionally for the people they are. Looking at your own emotional baggage and your own childhood can help you identify patterns and stop them repeating in your relationship with your own children. This can be deep work, and it can help to be facilitated in this by a counsellor. The work you do on yourself to process your childhood wounds and traumas can ripple out like a wave to affect the whole family positively because you are divesting yourself of patterns that can be harmful to the way you parent your children.

In the question above you mention reacting to your teenager's behaviour. It is wonderful that you are in a place to see that reaction to the behaviour is a choice. That already is a position of power. The power is in not reacting and going within yourself to see what parts are triggered in you. You can then just be with these parts and allow the energy to flow through you. If you are getting triggered it is ok to excuse yourself from the immediate situation, become calm and them re connect with your teen. When you understand that your teen is most likely not behaving in that way to trigger you, you can be more compassionate towards them. Becoming more compassionate to yourself by realising that parts of you are triggered is also major progress. This is not to say that you don't challenge their behaviour or put in place some consequence, such as the taking away of a device, if necessary. Always calm yourself before you have these conversations and remember to set an intention for the highest good of all. It is so positive that you are aware of your reactions and that your goal is to improve the interaction between you and your teenagers. You can make great progress forward from this place and your children are lucky they have an engaged parent who is striving to be a better version of themselves.

My adult child no longer speaks to me. What can I do?

We understand this is a distressing situation for you. We would say there is always hope that this will turn around in time should you be willing to do the vibrational work towards it. It is important that you first understand the role that you played in the current state of play. We say this not to blame you but to ensure that you know you contributed to this dynamic. If you are feeling that you are a victim, you need to move away from this by thoroughly examining your role in the current impasse. Be open to seeing how your actions and words affected another.

A starting point may be to put yourself in your child's shoes, to empathise with their experience of events. A willingness to forgive and possibly to make amends can be helpful. There should be no blame or shame around this. The past is gone and cannot be changed but if you are willing it may well be possible to find a way forward together. You may need professional help with this. Be willing to work through your own issues around the current situation before approaching your child. It can mean that you are in a better position to move forward when you try to connect. Working through these issues with a professional can mean that you have released resistance and resentment around the situation which makes a better starting point. Oftentimes in these situations it can be easier to forgive another than it is to forgive yourself. It is a worthy goal to work toward self-forgiveness and self-acceptance for the peace it can bring you. It is a process as there may be old patterns that you may need to release before it can be achieved.

As we have described before it is a really good idea to write positive aspects of your child down. Aim for as many as you can write. It can be from a time when they were younger or currently. Try to mine the deep feeling that you have for your child. Look at this list every day. We also suggest you pray for your child and send them positive energy and love. This is an active process, and it has real effects. Practice these two things daily for at least 30 days before you reach out to reconnect with your child. Doing the vibrational work before the physical interaction will pay off dividends when it comes to re-establishing the relationship.

Be open and willing to any interaction or relationship your adult child is agreeable to. It is important to move forward on their terms. The have put boundaries in place because they have been hurt, and they are protecting themselves so any new relationship must be on their terms, and it is important to respect this. It may also be the case that they wish for no interaction whatsoever. If this is the case, it is essential that you respect their decision. We have described the processes above how you can actively love and appreciate your child independent of any physical interaction with them. We suggest you use those processes, not just for reconciliation, but rather as a way that you can love them even if they do not wish you to be in their life.

CHAPTER 19

Coping with loss and grief with help from your angels

I have recently lost a loved one. I feel so shaken and upended and feel like life will never be the same again?

We love you and are with you at this difficult time. There is no doubt that the death of a loved one can be an extremely destabilising experience. It can feel like the rug is being pulled from under your feet.

We will say that death is not the opposite of birth as the person goes on to exist on another non-physical plane. Your loved one is still capable of sending you messages and keeping you in their intentions and prayers when they are in the non-physical plane. In fact, they are a much more powerful entity because they have united with the whole of their being in the non-physical realm. We say this to let you know you can still communicate with them, and you will be heard.

We know that the absence of their physical form is distressing to you. If you can accept this as early as possible it can be helpful with the processing of your grief. We can reassure you that your loved one is in a state of bliss and powerful in the totality of their being. They do not wish you to be burdened with heavy grief. We do acknowledge that grief is a process that is not linear and can be difficult in the early stages. Do what you can to be compassionate to yourself and allow yourself to rest.

Life will be different without the physical presence of your loved one but knowing that they are existing on another plane can be helpful. We urge you to try to communicate with your loved one and see what happens. They are most certainly thinking of you and sending you love.

My child has died, and it feels like I no longer have a purpose in this world. Is there any way I can go on?

We want to know that your guides are working with you currently to comfort you. You are not alone. We see the massive anguish this causes, and our love goes out to you. For most humans, this is the absolute worst thing that could ever happen. It seems to defy the natural order of things when a child dies before a parent. This is a false premise as far as we are concerned. Every soul on reincarnating onto Earth, is shown their path in life before agreeing to come forth into the physical form. This was no exception for the soul that was your child. Every life no matter how short, impacts those around them massively. We know this was the case, as the love you have for your child is now overwhelming in grief.

It has been said that grief is just love with nowhere to go. We say that your love does have somewhere to go, because the soul that was your child exists, albeit on another plane. You can channel your love towards the soul that was your child, and they can receive it. The love that they send back is multiplied by hundreds, for that is the love and the gratitude they have to you for being their parent. If they could speak to you, they would say that you could never be apart from them because there are invisible cords of energy that unite you always. Now, like your angels, they remain in the non-physical domain firmly focused on you and beaming positive energy your way. This is where they will stay faithfully, until you become non-physical yourself. If you can accept that death is not the end, you can communicate with and have a relationship with them. Despite what your physical senses tell you, you have not lost them, but you have a gained another being, focused on you in love and dedication, from the non-physical plane.

Most of us guides have not been physical before so we cannot fully appreciate what it feels like to feel the loss of a beloved one and miss their presence. Our intention with our words is simply to bring you some comfort. We never wish to play down the suffering you are experiencing. We merely wish to show you that your beloved is existing in another plane and is focusing love and attention on you.

I feel very alone in life. My partner has died, and I have no family close by. Can you help me?

We hope that in reading this book so far you can begin to appreciate that you are not on your own anymore. You are not and have never been alone, for you have your guides and your higher being always focusing their attention on you. They are appreciating you and beaming love towards you. In time, when you can move towards more positive thought you may begin to feel the wellbeing that emanates from them. In the meantime, if you feel able you can try to complete some of the exercises in this book to connect with your higher being and your guides.

We know that death is not the end of life and that your partner continues to exist on another plane. We can assure you of his love and how he is also focused on you and helping you where he is. We wish to tell you he is always wanting to connect with you. He is more powerful in his non-physical form, and he is focused on you. He has not forgotten you nor will he.

We know there is a period of adjustment after the death of a loved one. We can appreciate the destabilising nature of the event and how it impacts you. We wish to say we are here to help also. Connect with us through talking and prayer and we promise you that we will help.

A relative has committed suicide, I am so shocked and overwhelmed. I feel so guilty too. Can you help me?

This is indeed a very difficult situation. For us we see that the wanting in your relative to transition to non-physical was stronger than the will to live. This was the result of a strong wanting and a longing for relief. For them, it may not be a tragic as you believe. You cannot know the course of their lifetimes, contracts and karma and how they have combined to bring about this moment. You cannot without the viewpoint of non-physical, ever appreciate this, nor is it your work to figure this out or to feel guilty or responsible.

Of course, we realise the suddenness and the shock of the situation can feel overwhelming to you. Your guides and your higher being are with you and beaming wellbeing to you currently. It can be helpful to pray for and to your relative, that is deceased. Gather those around you who are supportive and reach out for help yourself now too. There is no doubt that your relative reunited with their higher being on returning to source and felt the fullness of their entire being. It is guaranteed that you relative has reached a broader perspective now while they are non-physical. The learning and expansion their life brought about has added to their own expansion and that of the entire universe.

My parent has died and there has been an unequal distribution of their assets to others in my family. I feel sad that I have been left out of the will. What can I do?

We are with you and send you love. We understand how this could be very distressing for you especially if you think this is because your parent did not love you. We know this is not the case. It may have been something that your parent neglected or perhaps they were led by another family member to draw up the will.

Of course you have legal avenues open to you. Perhaps you could first think about what the state of mind of your parent was when completing the will. Was there external pressure on them. Had an illness left them with impaired cognition? Did they fully appreciate the impact that the will would have on the family?

It is then up to you to decide how you feel about the situation. Allow time as you are already grieving the death of your parent. Perhaps it is something that could be resolved with another beneficiary of the will if you were to have a conversation with them. Think about what you would like to receive before you do this. If you decide to take legal action weigh up the possible benefits and risks involved.

Please realise that none of this has any impact on the amazing and powerful human being that you are. You are a powerful creator, and we are very much appreciating you and beaming you wellbeing from our place in non-physical. Your deceased parent is with us in non-physical and is beaming wellbeing toward you also.

Do our pets have souls, and do they experience an afterlife? I am distraught after my dog died.

Yes, of course, they have souls or essence energy that is less evolved in consciousness than humans. It can seem that your pet is pure positive energy. This is because animals often carry much less resistance and are often in the vibration of love and joy. In this way they can be uplifting to humans whose vibration may be lower due to ego prominence and split energy. Your pet is an uplifter of your energy through their demonstration of unconditional love to you but also their remaining present in the now. Your pet can teach you much when you observe their capacity for presence, love and joy. In short, they bring high vibes.

It can be very difficult when a pet dies because you feel their loss so acutely. That wonderful effect that they had on you is now missing and it is very painful. Your pet has a soul or essence energy, and this does return to the source on dying. They go to their proper place in the universe after dying and that energy is existing on another plane.

CHAPTER 20

Angelic advice for challenging life situations

I am estranged from my family of origin because they have been abusive to me. The dynamic was so negative I had to cut ties with them. I feel the pain of not having family in my life even though I know this was the right decision. How can I move forward?

We are with you and send you love. It seems that you have come to a position of personal power by no longer allowing negative people and patterns toxically affect your life. The benefit of this is that you have begun to create what you would like to manifest in your life without deferring to the opinions and input of your family. You are also putting yourself first which strengthens your position when it comes to manifesting what you desire. In the past when you have sought to please other people it has split your energy and meant that your desires took longer to come to fruition. Split energy also means that you manifest things that you do not desire.

The position you have taken with your family is one of strength because you have seen the reality of the situation and decided to prioritize self-preservation over the need to please your family. You cannot be your authentic self in such a relationship so your energy will always be split. It took courage to take this stance, and you know that it is what feels right and good for you.

When you place your attention on the lack of something in your life you are simply attracting more lack. It may be the lack of an idealised version of family that you are mourning but this bears no resemblance to the reality of the situation of your own family. We say friends can feel like family and that you can create your own family of like-minded caring people around you. We know your desire is strong for this to occur. For this to happen you must take your mind off the lack of your family of birth. This means trying to get some good feeling going about general topics and waiting for the law of attraction to deliver you more good feeling thoughts. Focusing your attention on the type of friends and relationships you would like to attract contributes to the work of vibrationally pre paving your path. This is something that you can do that is pleasant to do and more importantly will yield results in the long term.

You have everything you need to create a life where you are supported at every turn by loving relationships. Your desire for this to occur has caused you to ask for it and so it is already created in vibrational form. You must try and move in the direction of it by thinking good feeling thoughts and allowing your vibration to rise.

A friend of many years has ghosted me. I am very upset and confused. Can you help me?

While this is upsetting for you, it is a matter of vibration. It is not personal even though it seems like it is. You and your friend have moved away from each other because you have become vibrationally incompatible. While you can create drama and blame the other person, nobody is to blame. The law of attraction draws like to like but you are not vibing on the same level anymore and so are not drawn together as you were before. Your progression on this issue will depend on your willingness to let go and to accept the situation as it is in the present moment. Acceptance is the path of least resistance and even if you can move gradually in this direction, you will find some relief.

We urge you not to investigate the why of the situation because there is no way you will be able to fully appreciate all the nuances of what has occurred. There are many subtle energetic nuances at play. Please avoid seeing yourself as the victim also, as this is not the truth of the situation and it will keep you stuck. Allow the situation to be as it is and move forward as best you can, knowing there are others that will be attracted to your new vibration that will be more compatible to you and that will help you with your growth and expansion. Trust the universe has your back in this situation. It is not personal and ultimately it is for your growth and expansion.

I am in a group of friends who are pleasant, but they are much better off financially than I am. This can be difficult when it comes to group activities because I cannot generally afford these activities. I sometimes make excuses so I don't have to go but this is getting awkward What can I do?

As we mentioned earlier no good ever comes out of comparing yourself to another human being. You are all unique and brilliant. Money is just a vibrational energy. The fact that these friends have more money than you, does not make them superior in any way. If we look at this in terms of vibration again, it does not mean that they are a higher vibration than you. It simply means they are better at allowing the gifts of the universe to flow to them.

When you feel you are not worthy to receive whether consciously or unconsciously then you are energetically pushing away what you desire. This can take the form of pushing away friendships and people that you feel may be better than you. If you feel the people in the group genuinely appreciate and care for you then the best path is honesty. You are a born uplifter, and you bring your high vibration and wonderful personality to the table which is a form of currency. Everything does not have to be transactional.

It would be important to work on your feelings around what you deserve to receive and let go of any blocks that tell you that you are defined by your income. Open to the reality of the universe which is abundant and wants for you what you desire for yourself. Use affirmations to become more willing to receive. This energetic work is important so you can be open to receiving more but also so you can see the blessings that you already have in your life. This group of friends may be a blessing, or not, only you will know this. Look inwards and ask yourself are they a vibrational match to you. If so, then being honest will yield most dividends. If you feel that they are not a match, then it is ok to let the friendship go but first work on your perceptions and energy so that what you are believing is not a projection of your ego. Sitting quietly and feeling into your heart when doing this work is important. Decide from a heart level with compassion for yourself and your friends. It is important to realize that everyone is just simply where they are at in terms of vibration. The law of attraction will bring those that are alike together.

I have attracted a serious illness. Am I to blame?

No there is never blame from us because it could not exist at our vibrational level, nor should you blame yourself because this is a low vibrational emotion and it will not help. Yes, everything that shows up in your existence you have co-created with the universe. This is not to suggest you consciously co- created it, your own subconscious negative beliefs can cause this. The subconscious mind has a massive bearing on what you attract and so this can be a factor. Other factors include karma from past lives and soul contracts that you made before this incarnation. There are other factors would be too complex to understand at your current vibration that can be at play. Therefore, never blame yourself for what manifests. Go forwards using your guidance system to discern the best course of treatment and remember to keep healing as your highest intention daily.

The flip side of the law of attraction is that you do have the personal power to create what you desire in your life. You can do this through focus, intention, appreciation and keeping your vibration as high as possible. This is of course good news, and it can help you to realize that anything that you desire is possible. We promise you that this law is always working and is dominant very much like the law of gravity. It is always this way. If you can understand this, you can work towards putting it to use in your personal life. This is our ultimate message which is that you have great personal power, and you can truly have everything you desire in your life.

I am in a minority group, and I am angry at the injustices when it comes to inequalities in health, housing, resources, wealth and lifetime opportunities. How can I move through these feelings?

It is perfectly understandable to feel this way and the things that you point to are real issues and can seem overwhelming. We say this as gently as possible that no good can come from you focusing on these issues because what you focus on expands and becomes bigger in your experience. We say this not to deny the problem and certainly if you can take aligned action to advocate for yourself then you should do so, we merely speak the truth when it comes to the laws of the universe. If you can take your focus off these issues and place it on anything that you can appreciate in the moment. You can allow your vibration to rise and move away from being stuck in the vibration of anger and resentment.

We would like to say that often when a minority is supressed and discriminated against that there can be residual resentment and anger which can keep your vibration low which in turn can lead to the attraction of more of the same. We realise this is in no way just, nor do we say this not to apportion any blame. We simply wish to explain how the pattern continues and is enhanced.

We realise this information in this form can sound very triggering and potentially maddening. This not our intention. We wish to add no more distress to that which has already been inflicted. We feel that you can operate better when you are aware of the laws that govern your world. This knowledge is powerful and can impact your life and so we choose to speak it to you in the best words we can find. Please acknowledge and accept where you are at now, then use the processes we describe in this book to raise your vibration.

Many have mentioned righteous anger which can arise when you are hurt by another. We say that it is important to feel this anger in your body and move to allow it to expand and then watch it dissipate. It is true that holding anger in your body when you have repressed it can be bad for your health. Do not move to forgive anyone until you have fully felt and integrated this anger or resentment will arise later.

I am an addict, and I have burnt all my bridges in life. My family no longer speak to me, and I have lost all my possessions. I am still unable to stop using. I have lost all hope for the future and am simply existing. Can you help me?

We want you to know that you are a powerful creator of your world and you can make changes. Indeed, the addiction may be serving as a balm to soothe you from emotional pain and trauma from your life. While society might not endorse your choice it may simply be the one that means you can cope with life as it now is. Of course, we know that you are clever enough to realise that the mechanism you use to cope is unfortunately profoundly damaging to your body, your life and your relationships.

Is it possible to seek and get help to get sober and start living life again? Ask yourself and be honest "do you really want to continue living in this world"? We ask that in some cases addiction can be a way for people to end their lives when they have given up all hope. We do not believe you to be at this stage because even by asking us you are saying that you would like to change your life circumstances. It is important to acknowledge your intentions as your energy is split when you are acting from opposing objectives. Even if you are feeling suicidal there is help available to help you move from this negative state.

We want to reassure you that by wanting things to be different to how they are you have energetically created a different more fulfilling future. This has happened and is in existence. The work with the law of attraction is to move closer to what you desire by coming into a higher vibration by appreciating anything that you can. You can do this easily if this is a subject that regularly makes you happy. It will be easier to come to a higher vibration and then generate ideas on how to move forward and get help for your addiction. We say the inspiration will flow more easily when in this place.

There are those who can help you and they exist, and they are willing. If you can move slowly towards reaching out for help once you feel you are ready to stop using substances. Even if you cannot contemplate that now, always remember that there are those who want to help you and that help will be available to help you when you are ready to seek it. Whole organisations exist on this basis and there are thousands of people would have gone through this journey that are available to help. There may be those in your family who have not closed the door to helping you also.

A motivating factor might be to intend finding peace away from the constant pressure to get drugs and alcohol to feed your addiction. Can you imagine how peaceful your life would be if that tyranny did not exist. Of course, becoming sober will most likely mean facing your wounds and trauma. They ultimately exist despite you running away from them with numbing through taking substances. There is help and support to get you through this process and processing these traumas can leave you freer in the long run.

Your angels and guides have not forgotten about you, and they continue to beam wellbeing towards you. They know you as your highest and most powerful self and see not your addiction. They see only your infinite wellness and power to be, do and have what you want. They will never see you as you see yourself as an addict. They are focused on your potential and the amazing life you have created vibrationally. This is what they want for you.

I lately had an experience in nature that was beautiful and opened me up to the possibility that we are connected in ways I never appreciated before. I also felt much closer and compassionate to other people after having this experience. I have been a liar and a grifter all my life and have knowingly stolen from others. My past is not sitting well with me, and I am ashamed. Can you help me?

We are so happy that you have had this moment of expansion of consciousness in which you were profoundly changed. This is a wonderful thing that has happened, and it will shape your life and your experience going forward. It is not helpful to look back to the past because your power is in the present moment. You have become aware in the present moment of events that took place in the past that you are not proud of. There is most likely not a human alive that does not have some regrets about what they have done in the past. It is ok to forgive yourself for this now. Simply say the words I am willing to forgive myself for whatever it is. If you want and it is possible, you can make amends to a person you may have hurt in the past, only if it is feasible. It may help to know that you were doing your best with the consciousness you had at the time and now that you know better you will do better. Resolve now to honour nature and your fellow humans and align your action to this going forwards.

I am terminally ill, and I know I will die soon but I am having a hard time accepting it. I am bitter and resentful about my situation and angry with everyone. I don't want to spend my final months like this. I want life to be harmonious and to spend what time I have left with my loved ones. Please, can you advise me?

We have said before that all of you have a soul contract that details the length and nature of your life on reincarnating back to Earth. We know for a fact that you agreed to have this experience of illness at this time exactly as it is. It is challenging you and bringing up emotions that need to be healed before you either heal or make you transition to non-physical. This is as it should be. It is ok to experience these emotions and allow them to pass through you. Behind them is a well of peace so vast that if you could appreciate it, you would be so comforted. If you can allow these emotions to be as they are, then they will pass through. Your loved ones understand your apparent anger and frustration because it is a challenging situation for all concerned. If you can share how you are feeling with them it can help them be more aware of where you are coming from. If not, talking with a counsellor can be helpful to process how you are feeling. Even writing things down can be helpful because that is away of shifting the energy around the situation. Studies have shown that writing when angry can help diffuse the emotion.

It can also be helpful to write down and set some intentions for the next period of your life. If you have some burning desire perhaps you can make plans to achieve it. It can be helpful to write down what you wish to say to your loved ones before you go. Planning for your worldly goods to be passed on is also important. When it comes to intentions you mentioned wanting things to be harmonious. You can set an intention for this every day. If you can go more general and find things you appreciate in the moment this can open the gate for more joy to flow into your life. Be gentle with yourself and allow yourself to experience the full range of emotions. We are with and you are exactly where you are supposed to be in this time and space continuum.

We will be with you at the time of your passing so it may help to intend how you would like your final moments to unfold. Intending peace and harmony can be helpful. Remember death is not an end and you will simply be returning from whence you came. Of course, there may be fear involved but visualise your guardian angel and ask them for help with this process. The love that your family have for you will surround you and comfort you in your last days and then you will pass gently into the arms of the angels.

My parent was an alcoholic, and he abandoned my family physically, financially and emotionally. He has come back to the area I live in now and he wants to reestablish a relationship with me. He continues to drink and is chaotic, I have so much rage and anger towards him, and I don't see any change in his behaviour, nor do I see any will to atone on his behalf. There is a part of me that wants to help him, but I don't know what to do?

We want to acknowledge the amazing bright and beautiful being that you are. Even though this man was not present in your life you have survived and thrived. You are emotionally conflicted on this problem. We say you do not have to allow the person into your life. You have no obligation to do so. Your highest obligation is to yourself and your own wellbeing. If this man will offer nothing to you then it is ok to not engage or set boundaries about how you will engage with him.

Spend time thinking about what you would like to happen if you were to interact with him. Also, what would you want to get out of the relationship if you were to reconnect. It is a good idea to ponder what interaction he is capable of if he is engaged in active addiction. Your life was profoundly affected by his abandonment of you and your family. All feelings you have about him are valid and to be accepted as they are. Take time to reflect before engaging and realising that he may not be capable of the interaction you desire.

We want to keep yourself first and foremost in this process. There is nothing owed to this parent and engagement should be on your own terms. Do not be afraid to seek help as this situation is bringing up complex feelings for you whether through counselling or chatting it through with friends. Your obligation is to yourself and keeping yourself on an even keel. You decide if you engage with him, and if so on what terms. To some this may seem uncharitable, but we say that he is responsible for his vibration and his current state of being as are you for yours. It is wise to consider what effect interaction with him will have on you before engaging. Ask yourself to what end also for it is likely you will not be able to solve his problems. He has chosen this way of being and may not even see it as problematic. Go gently and listen to your inner voice and take your time.

I have recently become consciously aware of some painful events that happened in my childhood that I have been blocking out of my mind. It is very painful in my mind but also in my body which has started to seize up and become intensely painful. What can I do now?

We understand this is very difficult for you. The physical manifestations that are happening right now are your body's way of replaying events from your childhood trauma. It is a form of processing, and it may take a few days to complete. We suggest you take rest and surrender to it now. As challenging as this may seem, it is the path of least resistance. Go to bed and rest and allow what arises to be there. Your body needs you to witness this experience and be present as much as you can, of course if you feel you need medical help please seek it. It is our contention that this is a natural process, and it is coming up to be healed, at a time you can bear witness to it. Give yourself permission to be present and to grieve what was lost.

The body can protect you by holding on to the physical remnants of past traumas. Trust that the time is right for this to come up now and make space for it. By giving it time it will work its way through you. If you ignore it, it will surface again in its current form or in the form of an illness. The body is seeking to be heard right now, and you must listen. Afterwards, seek any support you can in the form of counselling, alternative therapies or medical care. Allow yourself to be supported by your loved ones.

Audrey has had to take to the bed on one occasion when relieving a trauma in her life she was overwhelmed. The withdrawing from her daily life gave her time to process what had happened on a physical level. It allowed her time to allow the sensations and emotions arise and to move through her. She allowed herself to cry and move in any way that soothed her. At times her hair was wet from crying, and her body ached from spasming. Audrey still thinks of that time as a sacred time of transmutation. It was exceptionally difficult, but it was also profoundly empowering because she had stopped running and had given her body space and time to heal. We are proud of her for being able to face it and to allow herself time and grace to process it.

Your angel guides are with you currently, and they are beaming love towards you. We are focused on the bright and wonderful future you have ahead and all the wonderful future events and things you have created that will flow to you in time.

CHAPTER 21

Your Intuition is your guiding star

How do I make decisions that are in alignment with my whole being including my higher being?

This is an important topic that we are glad you asked about. It is true that you have come into this world with an inbuilt guidance system. Your emotions let you know how you feel on any topic. It is often the case that some of you have a pattern of overriding this guidance system. This is conditioned behaviour which parents and society have imposed. For example, it is often imposed on females that they should be the good girl and that pleasing others is more important than pleasing themselves. This has led to negative situations in Audreys life where she overrode her internal guidance that told her that she should be wary of an individual. We say this not to blame her for she was blameless. Certainly, manipulation and an imbalance of power were at play. In retrospect, she would say that there were red flags which she ignored whether out of politeness or the desire to be liked. This second guessing of the self is indeed not without consequence. The most important message she teaches her children now is to respect that instinct and never question it.

Being more selfish by focusing on your desires

In relation to pleasing yourself we wish you would be more selfish. There is much resistance in the average person in relation to this concept. To co create with the universe and manifest your desires, it is important to have a clear focus on what you want and to keep your attention there. If being selfish is keeping your focused on your desires, then we wholeheartedly support this. This is not to say that if you can help another person, you can't do so. However, do not put their wishes and desires above your own as this will lead to discontent.

It is very important to examine the vibration you are at and your intention before going to help another. If sympathy for them is your predominant emotion the action you take will not be as helpful as if you were operating out of the intention to uplift the other. This is why acting out of a sense of obligation is not often aligned action because there is a split energy there. The will to help is opposed by resentment and so any action that comes from this state will not be as powerful.

We wish to speak of those of you who always put others before themselves in life. This may seem to you as an honourable position, and we do not doubt that you intend good when you take this position. We would just like to say that your creative power is dimmed in this position because you are working against the law of attraction, a most powerful law that determines what shows up in your life. You have left your position as one who can focus and manifest their desires. By putting the other person's desire above your own you split your power. Your message to the universe is that their desire is more important than your own. What is more, you broadcast the signal that your desires and expectations are not important. Thirdly when you put yourself in the position of the martyr your expectation is lessened as you have broadcasted that your desires are less important. This in turn dampens your attraction powers. Therefore, be selfish about your desires and keep focus on them and realise that you cannot help others and certainly not yourself by maintaining a position of split energy. It will keep both of you stuck.

A key to manifestation of anything you desire is having clear and focused energy on it. For many topics such as money your energy is split. This is because there may be many negative beliefs in contradiction to the desire to have more money. These may be deep seated beliefs that go back to childhood. It is always worth working through these beliefs and shifting them as this directly reduces the opposing energy that you have against your desire.

Another example of this is a person in a relationship who has the desire to leave a married partner. They may be clear on this desire yet have many conflicting beliefs that counter this desire. For example, they made a vow which must be kept, and that getting divorced would negatively impact their children. The desire for freedom is strong on one hand but the conflicting beliefs are offering strong resistance. An addition hampering factor is putting other's needs before the self. This is how many people find themselves becoming stuck in life situations and with people that no longer serve them

A way of overcoming such a dilemma would be to keep very clear on your desire and making your intentions to include freedom, alignment to the self and harmony. These intentions can be stated everyday no matter what the other is doing or how the situation is looking. An important part is to work through all the negative beliefs and release them. This is an ongoing process. By keeping focused on your intention for harmony you can stay in alignment with yourself and your desires no matter what the other is doing. By refusing to be triggered by events and keeping your focus on the best possible outcome for the family you may be able to shift the other persons perspective. Even if this is not possible, it will not matter because you have not lost alignment with yourself (your higher being) and you are in a powerful position. The likelihood of your will prevailing in this situation is much higher because you have maintained this position of power.

Why has my desire not yet manifested?

In fact, it can be worth looking at any desire that has not yet manifested in your experience and look at your contrasting views to it. Many of these may be held at a subconscious level so it is a good idea for you to write them down at a time when your mind is clear. Allow anything that occurs to flow onto the page. You may be astonished to learn of the subconscious blocks or opposing beliefs that you have. You can then work on letting these blocks go by just setting the intention to do so. Writing affirmations that are in opposition to your blocks can also be very helpful. This is a component that many law of attraction teachers omit to teach. It is not as simple as having a desire and putting it out into the universe. The following must be present

- Ask yourself what your vibration is like or what is your predominant emotion. The higher the vibration or emotion the better and this can be a good time to set an intention. Conversely if you are feeling not at your finest it is not a time to forward plan.
- Focus is incredibly important. We cannot overstate this. In general, the average person's focus is split in so many directions daily. This leads to split energy with your energy going in opposing directions. If it is difficult to keep focus on what you want this will slow down the manifestation of it.
- Consistency. It is important to have a consistent practice of meditation for example. This is because of the momentum you can generate on any given subject when this is the

case. It is important to consistently decide and place emphasis on what you desire in any moment.

- Being specific. It is important to be specific when setting intentions or asking the universe for something. It always a good idea to employ your senses when imagining what it will be like. Feel the feelings you will feel, what can you see, taste, hear, touch and smell. Once you have an idea of the feeling it can be a good idea to intensify this as much as possible.
- Surrender. It seems contradictory what we have said about focus and then we encourage you to surrender but it is not. Once you have set your intentions or put your desires out to the universe it can be a good idea to detach from the wish and take your mind off it. This is because trying to figure out how it will manifest and keeping a narrow focus on it can delay it coming to you. By doing this you are limiting your expectations and deliberately keeping yourself small. Surrender it to the higher power and it will come when you are ready for it.
- Acceptance/Allowance. We would say your wish is vibrationally granted as soon as you ask for it. Where you are on your manifestation journey is evidence in how your life looks right now. There will be many things that you have asked for that have not yet come into your experience. This is because of your willingness to allow them. We are aware that many will feel very angry at us for this statement, but it is completely true. You can, in fact, repel your desires by unconscious patterns and negative thought. The most common one that we see is that you are feeling undeserving or unworthy. Almost every one of you to some degree feels this way. This is sometimes because of childhood conditioning or societal input, but it is very real. The newborn baby does not doubt his worthiness and will not settle for less than he needs.

> In a world where it is frowned upon to be selfish you have absorbed so many messages of guilt and unworthiness. It is in questioning those beliefs, even the hidden ones and reversing that conditioning that progress can be made to feel more worthy. Keeping yourself on a high vibration and working towards self-love and feeling worthy are very important in changing what you can bring into your life.

Appreciation of the life that you already have is also key to bringing in more desires as if your energy is split noticing what you do not like it can also impact your ability to manifest. We wish to tell you that everything that you wish to live, and all your desires have already been granted in energetic form. Ask yourself how willing you are to let them come to you. Can you work on your resistance that is keeping your metaphorical wall up to stop what you want flowing to you? Finally, we say this not to blame because there is none of that. We appreciate that you are already whole and complete and are a magnificent creator. There is nothing that you are doing wrong but we want you to feel the worthiness of your being and allow what you have already requested to flow into your experience.

People have written hundreds of books, indeed some assisted by us, as is this book, about the secrets of manifestation. It does not need to be complicated. We tell you if you follow our processes consistently with focus you will notice things you desire showing up faster in your life. It is meant to be a fun and light-hearted exercise and seeing it that way also can be helpful.

Does everyone have a guidance system that is alignment with their higher being? Does everyone then suffer when there is a disparity between the two? Have some people completely overridden their guidance system?

Yes, everyone has this inbuilt guidance system from birth. Everyone experiences feelings when they are not alignment with their higher being. These feelings are predominately negative. There is of course a chance to catch them early. Discomfort and suffering result from momentum from negative feelings accruing from acting in opposition to your higher being (ignoring instincts). It is an almost universal experience that some suffering comes from being out of alignment with your higher being. As most are completely unaware of this mechanism their suffering can persist. Part of this mechanism is what you would call your conscience or moral code. Feelings of negativity can result from acting in opposition to this mechanism.

As mentioned most are unaware of the existence of their higher being and the totality of their being. The conscience acts to alert you as to how you are aligned with your higher and whole self. Of course, there are many who override this instinct. The mind can be used to justify all actions. There are also many who are cut off from their guidance system through excessive mental activity and general distraction or numbing. Unfortunately, the negative feedback from non-aligned actions comes to them anyway. Some will use this as evidence of them being a victim while others will disconnect even more from their guidance system. It often comes to a stage where they are acting out their mental patterns with no input from their guidance system. This can lead to more negativity and feelings of victimhood. There is a positive feedback loop where people gain recognition and material rewards from their bad behaviour. This can act to compound this pattern too. Those narcissists and sociopaths among you are noted to have no moral compass and it is believed by society that they suffer not the ill effects of their bad deeds. We would like to say that this is not true. They do suffer as they are not in touch with their whole being as a result do not have that power of attraction. From the outside they may look like they are getting away with their misdeeds, but you cannot see the ways that they will pay through karma and future lives. We can see the bigger picture and can report they will suffer immediately or suffer later but they will suffer.

It is not simply about doing the right and moral thing acting in alignment to your higher being is the path of least resistance. It is the position that maximises your power to create. In this position of following your guidance and becoming aligned with your higher being (through meditation or being in the moment) you multiply your power exponentially. Good ideas start to flow to you, and you are energised to take steps that can make all the difference on your path to creating the life that you desire. When you are in alignment you are one with the flow of life. The momentum can move you closer to manifesting your desires into matter.

A typical pattern may be allowing another person's behaviour to influence your general mood and vibration. We say allowing because this is something you allow, and you do not have to do so. If you can take your attention off the subject of the other person and how they are affecting you, it will be possible to begin to get a little relief. Taking your attention from the subject can be freeing on many levels. When you take your attention off it you remove the power of another to affect you. Raising your vibration through positive thought can help you come to conclusions and act from a place of power. This is planning with consideration to the whole of you, with the resources of your higher being. Positive and aligned actions must follow from this place of power and the situation is more likely to be resolved in a way that will benefit you.

Is there any message that you have, to help us with our daily lives?

The main one is that we wish you would be easy about things and take your mind off conditions and things that are bothering you. As you give you attention to negative subjects they gain momentum. It must be so as it is law (the law of attraction). So, it is always best to take your mind off those topics that cause you to feel negatively. If you can begin to take note of anything positive and expand the feeling of positivity. It can be a place in your body that feels safe and warm. If you are still in bed in the morning it can be the feel of the sheets and the pillow against your skin. It can be taking time to notice some small items that surround you. It is not about distraction but finding some small thing that pleases you and then them enhancing the feeling of pleasure so you can move up the scale slowly towards more pleasant feelings. It can take time to get momentum behind the feeling so do not expect to go from side of the coin to other instantly. It doesn't have to be difficult. It can as easy as looking for a better feeling thought and moving from there. Also taking your attention off what does not serve you such as the constant negative news cycle.

CHAPTER 22

Cultivating abundance with the angels

What can you tell us about expectation and the process of creation/manifestation?

It is true that most people get what they expect as opposed to what they desire. You are programmed by society and family what to expect from life. Indeed, you are conditioned to lessen expectations in order not to be disappointed. This process starts when you are young and continues throughout life. Many people in their middle years are living miserably, in the lives their parents wanted for them, never asking what they want for themselves. Also never giving themselves permission to break away from the prison they are in. Many put off living their desired lifestyle for a later date such as retirement or when they have more money or some day off in the future. Not everyone reaches this point, and many may not be in good health to enjoy it.

We ask that you be easy with yourself and allow yourself to dream that things can be different. Take a little space and time to reflect and follow your instincts. It is true that when you take a leap of faith to follow the life that you desire the universe supports you and often new opportunities come to you. It all comes back to allowing yourself. Allowing yourself the time to reflect. Allowing yourself to do something that interests you. Perhaps taking one day a week off to pursue what really matters to you. We of course are aware that you have obligations financial and otherwise and may not be able to change things as dramatically as you would desire. That is ok, just take a little time to meditate and focus on what you desire. This is putting out positive intention into the universe, and it will come back to you in the future. Hold the faith that you are working towards your ideal existence and take little steps every day in that direction. These actions can have an enormous momentum in helping you move towards where you want to be.

What is it you would like us to know about our ability to make changes in our lives?

We would say it is unlimited. We see you from a perspective of the totality of your being and it indeed a beautiful sight. You have been conditioned through life in this world to see yourself as small and limited. Your mental patterns also feed into this and many feel that they should believe their thoughts which may not be true or representative of their actual potential. We say that there are very few of you who have an objective view of your potential. You have been conditioned to focus on your lack and flaws and to think small. We can see your potential and if you can come a little way towards us in your beliefs, we know you can change your mind and with this change your life.

Your attention is a currency and at the present there are billion-dollar corporations competing for your attention at any one time. You ask how your attention can be valuable, but we say it is one of the most valuable resources that you possess. Like all resources it can seem finite, but we can tell you ways in which you can increase your attention span and use your attention in a way to benefit you. It is a law of the universe that what you place your attention on will expand. This is why we urge you to stay focused on those things that you wish to bring into your life. It is equally as important to take you mind off those things that you do not want to replicate in your personal situation. This is becoming harder because of the nature of modern distractions.

It is ineffective to have your focus spit in multiple different directions. Of course, there are those that do, but the split energy can lead to a diminished power to attract what you wish to manifest. If you focus on those things that make you happy this can expand your energy in the direction of your desires. Feeling good feeling emotions and keeping your focus on what is pleasing to you can result in a boost of energy for you. Conversely by placing your attention on negative thoughts it can lead to energy lost as negative thoughts are a lower vibration and the attention can multiply the negativity. Everybody already knows this because they feel it but not everyone is discerning of what they put their attention into. You can be taken off your positive path by negative conversations with friends or family, watching or reading the news, interacting with your phone or being carried away by negative thoughts to name but a few. It stands to reason then that caring about how you feel and about what you are giving you attention too is important. The exercise which we have described before in mapping where your energy is flowing will be highly beneficial here. There are certainly places where your energy is trapped that may no longer serve you. Thinking about this and creating the map can be the first steps to changing this and in freeing up energy for you to use elsewhere in your life. If possible, go back and have another look at this exercise.

I am very fortunate in my life circumstances. Is it wrong to want more?

It is wonderful that you are fortunate in your life situation which in no doubt has been brought about by your vibrational work whether conscious or not. It certainly the goal of life as we see it to have new desires and bring into existence conditions and circumstances that serve you. This is why you came back into this physical existence to hone your skill at having everything the way you desire it to be through becoming aware and proficient at using the predominate laws of the universe to your advantage. The basis of the universe is expansion, and your personal expansion benefits the expansion of the whole. This is true in what you perceive as negative and positive situations. Therefore, it is perfectly natural to want more and in no way wrong. This desire is the basis of everything that comes into your experience.

What you are describing in your question is a resistance or not allowing the flow of life. This is most likely through old beliefs and social conditioning. It is important to work to let these beliefs go as they are influencing what you can attract into your life. The main way this happens is that they slow down the time it takes for your desire to come to fruition after the instant creation in vibrational form. We have not done this before but will now describe how this happens. It is to do with the vibration that you are at when awaiting the creation to flow to you. Negative thoughts can change your density, vibration and antenna to detect that you are in the vicinity of what you desire. The upshot of this is poorer manifestation power and slowed down manifestation. When you create what you desire it is kept in vibrational form for you and cannot be uncreated, if you do not line up in the vicinity of it in this lifetime you will feel the benefit of it when you return to the non-physical realm.

I want more money how can I achieve this (is it even spiritual to want more)?

Firstly, there is no judgement from us or from source God in relation to what you desire. It is also true that what you desire desires you too and so it has been granted in an energetic form that has not yet turned into matter. We realise this sounds very frustrating to you especially if you are eager to accumulate more money, but it is factual.

Sometimes when you say you want more money the law of attraction emphasises the wanting of the money and highlights this and not the actual abundance. That is why it is more helpful to act like what you want is already in existence. Good affirmations in this line are Money flows to me easily. I am abundant and wealthy. The words "I am" are powerful as they are a representation of source God who describes themselves as "I am that I am". It is important never to put anything you don't want to attract after the words I am. Use the innate power of the I am to affirm what you do want. Of course, many of you when you say I am wealthy will have huge resistance and anger come up. Allow it to come up and work on letting it go.

Now you have asked for more abundance, and it has been given and has begun existence as an energetic or vibrational form. The speed at which these manifests in your life or turns into matter is directly related to a few factors. Expectation, your vibration, resistance to it in the form of money blocks or other beliefs and your ability to detach. Expectation is important as your desire can be killed in the early stages by being sceptical or doubting it. Another form of this is dictating how it should happen and not being open to the different ways it could manifest in your life.

Your vibration influences the process. It is important to be in the receptive mode. This can be affected by states of depression and intense fear for example. If you are resistant to the flow of abundance into your life even on the subconscious level, it can affect the outcome of this process. You are raised with many beliefs on money such as it being the root of all evil. If having large amounts of money is likely you to make you feel unsafe then it is logical that you would block it flowing into your life. It is always a worthwhile exercise to examine your beliefs around money and release them so you can welcome in more abundance.

There is another factor that we will talk about now and that is surrender. It seems counter intuitive but to maximise the power of what you manifest it is important to ask for what you want but then to detach from it. Surrendering your desires to greater intelligence or the universe makes your desires manifest quicker. In this you are not just using your own power to bring about your desires, but you now use the power of the universe to co-create it with you. You must truly detach and forget about it afterwards for this to be effective. It is important not to have one eye on it. For it to work you must detach by taking your attention off it.

We realise that this answer is multifaceted and may seem complicated. Take time to read over it and go through the processes mentioned above and then remember to detach from it.

Here are some affirmations for abundance

I am abundant and attracting more to me all the time.
Money flows to me easily and effortlessly.
I trust that I am taken care of by the universe and all my needs are provided for.
Money is an energy that I welcome into my life.
I expect it and then I receive it.
I am truly grateful for the abundance I am receiving in my life.
My abundance is flowing to me now and I am grateful.
I deserve to receive all the abundance of the universe.
I am deserving of anything my heart desires that is for the highest good of all.
I love money and money loves me in return.
My abundance is created and assured and is flowing to me now.
I am a powerful creator and can create the conditions I favour in my life.

CHAPTER 23

Final Words

Some positive developments- Collective Consciousness and humanity

The good news is that connecting with your angels can have a knock-on effect for the rest of the world. In simple terms, this is a matter of vibration. To improve your chances of connection you will have to clear the clutter as described earlier. This, in effect, allows your vibration to rise so you are on a similar frequency to us. In raising your vibration, you are adding to the collective consciousness of the world and raising the frequency on the planet.

Despite all that you see to the contrary in the world the collective consciousness is rising in frequency. The contrast that you see in the world is having the effect of intensifying this progression. It is sweeping out all the dark corners which is why it can feel like there is a lot of oppressive heavy energy at play now. It can be hard to tolerate for empathetic or spiritually attuned people currently. It is wise to practice grounding, clearing and self-care practices to protect your energy. A rise in the consciousness of the individual influences the whole, because everything is interconnected.

It was our intention that there would be a vibrational shift in you, due to reading this material. Vibration is everything and this can bring about profound changes in your life and the life of others around you. We aim to uplift and comfort, and we hope our words have brought you some peace and solace.

In need of inspiration?

We have tried throughout this book, to give you the best words we can find so that you can appreciate yourself more. We appreciate you and love you so much just as you are. There is nothing you need change. You are beloved and appreciated by your guides in non-physical.

Instead of looking outwards to seek inspiration you can see you go within and find out all you need to know. You have the help of your higher being and your guides who wish to impart wisdom to you if you can listen.

Audrey sometimes receives inspiration after meditating. For example, if she was mulling something over the answer becomes clear afterwards. This is because meditation stops all resistance, and it allows the answer to occur to her. She is often in a more receptive mode too which makes the knowing instantaneous.

For everything you need to know and to develop in your life, the answers are found within. Your power is magnified when you seek the answers within and do the energetic work on what you want to manifest.

We sometimes send you messages or put people on your path. We can do this more easily when you make time for meditation and tuning in. The general population is receiving the messages in about 1% of cases only due to them being tuned to other sources. With those with whom we have worked, this increases dramatically. We will keep trying in every case anyway, but we know that it will help to get our message out as there will be more of you who will be willing to listen. Regardless of whether you interact with us or not we will always remain in non-physical appreciating you and beaming love towards you.

What do angels want for you now?

We are so grateful that you have taken the time to read this book. We wanted to bring our viewpoint to a wider audience and to reassure you that you are loved and you are cherished by your non-physical angels and guides. We want you to use us as a resource and to be aware that you have the benefit of existing as a larger being than your eyes can see. Your higher being is the greater part of you and is equipped with the benefit of the wisdom and knowledge of all the lives that you have lived. This is a tremendous resource. Even if you never connect with us or with your higher being, you have the power to choose thoughts and emotions that feel good and that this is the fastest path to having the life you desire.

We want you to know that you are a treasured part of all of creation and any steps that you take to become more conscious are helpful to the whole of the universe. There is no rush with this, and you have not missed the boat nor are you behind in any way. You can choose to move forward by focusing on the best feeling thoughts and by trying some of the processes and meditations listed in this book. It is our assertion that you have been changed by reading this book. It has impacted your vibration in addition to your soul which has been brought to a remembering of its worth and its power.

Peace and clarity are positive goals to aspire to. When you have clarity, it can make life much easier. Your decisions flow as you have the answer immediately. Of course, it is important to be discerning about what you are receiving in guidance and take only what resonates with you. When you move forward using your innate guidance your foot is steady on the path and your way is clear. You are beloved. You are powerful and you can create the life that you desire with the full and loving support of your angels.

A final message from your angels.

Beloved ones you are so dear to us,
We want you to enrich your life by connecting with us.
We wish to give you clarity and encouragement.
It is our intention that you will be uplifted by our presence.
Look within and decide how you feel about our words.
We wish to bring you to a full remembering of the powerful and magnificent beings you really are.
Powerful and luminous beings, every one.
We are always with you and beaming love to you.
We send you much love and blessings, most precious ones, for you are unique. There is only one of you in the entire universe.
Right now, we ask that you reach out to us if you desire connection and we will shape and guide you.
There is nothing you cannot be, do or have,
Believe this and expect your good to flow to you.
You are most beloved and treasured by all of us on the non-physical plane.
Try to love yourself as we love you.
You are more precious to us than all the diamonds and precious metals in the world.
Beloveds we ask you to connect with us so we can co -create lovingly and joyously.
We are one and ALL IS ONE.

APPENDIX 1

AFFIRMATIONS

Remember it is important to say these affirmations when you have some positive momentum going and are feeling good. Repeat them regularly in the morning if possible. Remember writing them down is three times more powerful. You can also say them aloud.

HEALTH

I am healthy, whole and complete.
My body is upgrading and improving every day.
My cells are intelligent and autonomous, and they are creating a healthier me.
I am grateful for my body's innate wisdom.
Where my attention goes energy flows. I open my heart and send energy to the place in my body that needs it most.
I am healing little by little every day.
I now discard any beliefs that I have about my body that are not loving.
I love my body and appreciate all it does every day.
I am a vessel for love.

SAFETY

It is safe to be me.
It is safe to express myself as I choose.
My inner world is reflected outwardly. As I feel safe in my body, I am safe in my environment.
It is safe to express myself as I wish.
I am always safe, loved and protected.
My non-physical family and guides are watching over me.
It is safe for me to be seen in the world.
It is safe to be exactly as I am right now.

CREATIVITY

I am naturally creative, and I express myself easily.
Creativity is my natural way to exist in the world.
I was born with innate creativity which I now choose to express.
It is safe to create.
It is safe to express myself.
I am talented and have infinite ways to express my creativity.
Being creative is as natural as breathing.
When I stifle myself creatively, I am not in harmony with myself.
Creating for the joy of creating is my goal.
All my creations are beloved.

HARMONY

Harmony is my goal in my environment and my relationships.
Loving and harmonious relationships are my birthright.
I go within to seek inner harmony, and this is reflected in my outer environment.

I can intend harmony before all my interactions to ensure harmonious outcomes.
I am living in harmony with all those who are in my life.
I am living in harmony with Mother Earth.

PEACE AND SERENITY

I am peaceful and at ease in my life.
My relationships and life situation are peaceful and harmonious.
I go within to seek serenity.
I am calm, centred and serene and this is my natural state.

JOY

Joy is my birthright.
I am wired to experience joy in my life.
Joy is my default state.
I allow myself to experience more joy in my life.

MAGNETICISM

I am a magnetic person, and I easily attract people and circumstances that are for my higher good.
I attract others to me as I am magnetic and warm.
My high vibration draws others of a similar vibration into my life.
My personal power and high vibration are attractive to others

APPENDIX 2

Example of an energy map

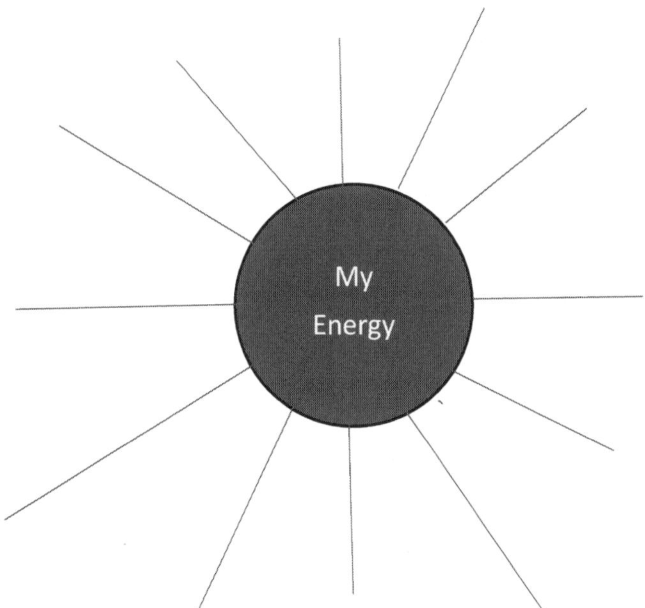

APPENDIX 3

References

References

Hawkins, Dr D, *Power vs Force,* (2013), Fifth Edition, Hay House.

Hicks, E, *Ask and it is Given,* (2012), First Edition Hay House.

Pathway Teaching, *Shamanic practitioners Medicine Wheel Manual*, (2014).

ACKNOWLEDGEMENTS.

I am so grateful to my angel guides for trusting me to bring their words to you. Jeronimo the scribe angels were responsible for me completing this book. I never take for granted how lucky I am to have to have the loving guidance of the angels in my life which has given me immense peace and clarity. I hope the words they have shared in this book will help bring you some comfort too.

I am grateful to have worked with some amazing healers to improve my health. I thank Aisling O Leary, Fiona Rooney and Kathy Cooney who have been profoundly impactful in this regard. I thank those who have helped me on my spiritual path, Melanie, Sylvia Parsons, Shauna Brady, and Paul O Halloran, among others. I am lucky to have found some lovely groups with similar interests. My gratitude to all members of the sea swimming, moon fire, Artist Way and Rahanni Celestial Healing groups I have been involved with.

Thanks goes to Vanessa Diaz of Balboa Press. I very much appreciate my husband Peter and my three wonderful children Sean, Darragh and Rosa. A big thank you to my first readers and very good friends Bridget and Caroline for their feedback. Much love to my wider family, friends and colleagues. Thank you for being there for me.

ABOUT THE AUTHOR

Audrey has been channelling guidance from her angels for over six years now. She has worked as a midwife and a nurse for many years. Audrey's interest in angels led her to become qualified as a Rahanni Celestial Healing practitioner and teacher. This is a heart centred energy healing modality that channels high frequency energy to promote healing. She has also qualified in Quantum Healing and has used both modalities in her therapy practice.

While working with people she receives images of their guardian angels and passes on angelic messages that are deeply meaningful to them. Audrey receives daily guidance from her angels, which has transformed her life, for which she is deeply grateful. Her angelic guides told her that she would write this book on the first day she began hearing their guidance. Audrey lives in the West of Ireland with her husband Peter and their three children.

Printed and bound by CPI Group (UK) Ltd, Croydon, CR0 4YY
05/05/2026
02102759-0005